How to Make the Most of your Psychology Degree

D1380477

How to Make the Most of your Psychology Degree

Study skills, employability, and professional development

Rachael Leggett, Daniel Waldeck, and Amy Burrell

Open University Press

Open University Press
McGraw Hill
8th Floor, 338 Euston Road
London
England
NW1 3BH

email: enquiries@openup.co.uk
world wide web: www.openup.co.uk

First edition published 2022

Comissioning Editor: Clara Heathcock
Associate Editor: Beth Summers
Content Product Manager: Ali Davis
Head of Portfolio Marketing: Bryony Waters

A catalogue record of this book is available from the British Library

ISBN-13: 9780335250882
ISBN-10: 0335250882
eISBN: 9780335250899

Library of Congress Cataloging-in-Publication Data
CIP data applied for

Typeset by Transforma Pvt. Ltd., Chennai, India

Fictitious names of companies, products, people, characters and/or data that may be
used herein (in case studies or in examples) are not intended to represent any real
individual, company, product or event.

Praise page

"A friendly and accessible guide to being a Psychology student, with advice on studying, professionalism, and future careers. This is an invaluable resource to making the most of your Psychology degree!"
Elisa Lewis, Lecturer in Psychology, London South Bank University, UK

"I am delighted to see this book being available for psychology students but also for those interested in studying psychology. It offers an excellent 360° perspective on the profession and the often confusing and intricate path to becoming a psychologist. The blended take on explaining psychology as a field and clear guidance on how to succeed in this profession make this book a required read for anyone at the beginning of this exciting journey. Comprehensive yet easy to follow, the book offers a clear and dynamic layout that should answer all the questions you have about psychology."
Eduard Daniel Margarit, Founding President Psychology Corner,
Chair BPS Student Committee

"'How to Make the Most of Your Psychology Degree' is such a pragmatic book, crammed full of highly practical and helpful tips and advice, that it will serve as a supportive guide for psychology students throughout their academic journey, not just at the beginning. The authors have chosen their illustrative examples and activities in each chapter wisely in that this book would readily serve as core reading content for undergraduate Psychology modules centred around building a student's research and study skills, project planning and management, employability, and personal and professional development and self-reflection. The wide variety of topics covered is a real strength, with key focus on developing the critical thinking essential for careers as an academic psychologist or scientist-practitioner."
Dr. Ian Tyndall, Reader in Cognitive Psychology, Institute of Education,
Social, and Life Sciences, University of Chichester, UK

Contents

1 How to use this book

Welcome to *How to Make the Most of Your Psychology Degree: Study skills, employability, and professional development*. Wow, that is a mouthful! – note to self, make sure the next book has a shorter title (or at least makes for an amusing acronym). We are delighted that you have picked this book up and are reading this introduction in your local bookshop, taking a sneak peek via an online retailer, and/or have actually purchased a copy. Before we get started, we thought it would be useful to give you a quick history of how the book came about, what we are aiming to achieve, and how you can get the most out of it. Hence this chapter entitled 'How to use this book'. Here, we set the scene for the book, explain how the book is structured (and why), and provide some tips for how to engage in the learning (in the most useful way for you).

Overview of topics

- Who is the book for?
- What is the book about?
- How is the book structured?
- How do I use this book?

Learning outcomes

1 To develop an understanding of how the book will aid you on your learning journey in Psychology
2 To understand how to use the book effectively

Who is the book for?

People about to start, or who are currently studying for, an undergraduate Psychology degree. Wow, section done! Phew that was easy – I wonder if the rest will be so straightforward …

What is the book about?

To help you understand where we are coming from, it is probably worth giving you a quick history of how this book came about. The authors (Rachael, Dan, and Amy) all teach in Higher Education and have, between us, taught hundreds (if not thousands!) of Psychology undergraduates. We find that students often struggle with the uncertainty of career planning and/or are worried about making the most of their degree. We have therefore decided to put together an easy-to-access guide for how to get into the right mindset for studying Psychology and how to make the most of your time as an undergraduate. There are many career opportunities that spring from a good quality Psychology degree and we hope to show you that, regardless of your background or interests, if you work hard and take the right approach, you can be successful. This book aims to support you to develop the skills to do this.

So, first and foremost, here are the key attributes you need as a Psychology student:

• An open mind
• The right attitude

That's it. Sounds easy doesn't it?! You think we are joking? Nope. But there are different ways to interpret the above, so let's unpick this some more.

What do we mean by an open mind?

There are lots of skills/attributes people think about when preparing for studying Psychology, such as empathy, patience, time management, problem-solving, reflection, commitment to learning, and so on. These are all good skills/attributes to have but, at the start of your degree, not something you need to worry about if you are not quite there yet (this is what we are here to help you with!). There is only really one thing you need to bring with you when you study Psychology and that's an open mind. What we mean by this is being open to new ideas. You don't have to agree with everything but learning to listen to other people's experiences and viewpoints helps us learn and to be better Psychologists. Remember, people are different, their experiences are different, their views are different, and so it is important to be open to listening to others. People will not always agree (and you will likely very strongly disagree with at least one person during your time at University), but it is important to listen to their arguments and, if you disagree, present an evidence-based (rather than emotional) rebuttal. Keeping calm and being open and non-judgemental is fundamental to understanding people – which is, ultimately, what all Psychologists want to achieve.

It is also worth saying that, contrary to popular belief, Psychology is not an 'easy' subject. It can be hard to get your head around at times, especially in a world where there are so many individual differences (e.g. how can you apply one theory to all people and circumstances?). Thus, you need to be prepared for situations where there is no 'right' answer. Remember, we work with probabilities and test hypotheses and so you are more likely to hear Psychologists talk about the weight of evidence for or against a theory rather than 'proof'. Thus, whilst Psychology is evidence-based, you will need to learn how to critique the quality of evidence and consider alternative viewpoints. You'll also need to be prepared to learn how to argue your case.

What do we mean by the right attitude?

To be successful at anything in life you need to apply yourself. Studying for a Psychology degree is no different. You can't just sit back and expect the degree to land on your lap. You need to take a proactive approach and engage fully in the learning throughout your degree (no slacking off at the end of term or in first year because 'it doesn't count'). In short, you should always strive to be an active learner with the emphasis on *active*! We don't just mean turn up on time for classes but also *engage* in these sessions. For example, answer the questions the tutor throws out to the room, take an active role in group work, and take opportunities to develop your skills when they arise (e.g. volunteer to be the nominated group member to feed back to the class). And don't just think about what your degree offers you. Think about the other opportunities your University has – for example, are there options to study abroad? What work experience is available? Can you develop another skill (such as a language) alongside your degree? You don't have to be involved in everything (in fact, we recommend you don't as you won't have time to study!) but picking out a few core extra-curricular activities will boost your skills development and help you stay motivated.

Having the right attitude also extends to how you interact with others. Remember it is not the lecturer's job to ensure you pass, that is your responsibility. Tutors are there to support and guide you and, importantly, we want you to pass (thinking about it cynically, who wants the resit marking?!!) but we also have standards to maintain. We are not obliged to pass you (no matter how much money you pay in fees) and we won't if the work is not up to scratch. We will help you, we will signpost you, we will support you. But getting that good grade? That is up to you. You should take responsibility for your own learning right from the very beginning (reading this book is a good start) and not be afraid to put in some hard work.

Before moving on to how the book is structured and how to use it, it is worth outlining what the book is not … so that we set your expectations appropriately!!

What this book is not

First, the book is not an exhaustive resource about Psychology. If you want to read about Milgram's prison experiment or understand why Pavlov's dogs salivate, you need to go and read the research literature on these topics. It is also not a fully comprehensive overview of all the many career paths you can take with a Psychology degree – basically, don't assume that if you don't see your ideal job in these pages that particular option is not open to you. Psychology is about people. Psychology is about behaviour. There are plenty of roles that we don't talk about that are legitimate options for you. However, if you do find something that you are interested in that we don't mention, we hope this book will help you understand how to apply your Psychology skillset to your chosen career. In sum, although this book is about Psychology, it is not particularly Psychology topic focused. It is much more about the journey of studying Psychology (with some interesting Psychology examples along the way). We hope that makes sense. And you still want to keep reading ...

How is the book structured?

The book is broken down into topics. Each chapter centres around knowledge or a skill that we feel is vitally important for you to understand. These are as follows:

Chapter 2: Why Psychology?
Chapter 3: The British Psychological Society and career pathways
Chapter 4: Professionalism
Chapter 5: Learning from experience and digesting feedback
Chapter 6: Research methods: why are they important?
Chapter 7: Effective research strategies and utilising the library
Chapter 8: Academic integrity and referencing
Chapter 9: Critical thinking
Chapter 10: What next?

Each chapter is designed to provide an overview of why each skill is important and provide tips to help you get started and/or to continue to develop the skill. We strive to help set expectations for your course so you know what you are likely to be asked to do and give you some insights to help get you started (and hopefully reduce the likelihood of you feeling overwhelmed).

Each chapter has learning outcomes to help you understand what you can get out of reading the chapter. We also provide 'thinking space' and/or activities within each chapter to help you think about what you have learned. It is worth saying at this point that this book is designed to be written in, highlighted, and scribbled all over! Even if you have an e-book copy we hope you'll be able to add comments or keep a record of your thoughts alongside the book. Please use the book in any way you like. We hope that this helps you to engage with the text in a way that supports your own individual journey.

How do I use this book?

Okay, let's not beat around the bush here. We are aware that some people choose Psychology as they don't really know what they want to do. Others choose it because they are fascinated by people and/or know exactly what career they want. Both are fine and you can all achieve a good quality degree and go on to do amazing things. You are all on your own individual journey and will be at different stages of that journey. With this in mind, please don't feel limited by the traditional approach of reading a book from cover to cover. You can do this if it is what you prefer but you don't need to. For example, if you are new to Psychology and still figuring out what you want to achieve, reading this book cover to cover might be a useful approach. However, if you have a good idea what you want to do, have particular questions you want answered, and/ or skills you want to focus on, then do dip into chapters that are of particular interest to you. Remember, you can also come back to specific chapters at a time when they are more relevant – for example, you might want to read the academic integrity and referencing chapter before handing in your first assignment, or the digesting feedback section once you have your first set of results.

For our part we have added signposts between chapters so, if you are dipping in and out, you can see how other chapters relate to what you are reading. We are also conscious that some people prefer learning from visual sources and so will provide advice and/or signposts to visual learning options where we can. As you have probably gathered already, our aim is to provide information in a chatty, informal style. We hope this makes the content more accessible for you and easier to pick the book up to read/re-read content. This does not mean it is not based on good quality information though! We have researched the book in depth and have ploughed years' worth of our own (and colleagues') experiences and tips into it. We hope you find it useful.

Activity 1.1

What do you want to get out of reading this book? Just jot down a few thoughts here. Come back to this later (once you've read a few more chapters) and review it (i.e. are you getting what you want out of reading the book?).

2 Why Psychology?

Psychology is an exciting and varied science! In this chapter, we will explore what Psychology is, who Psychologists are, and how we might use Psychology in everyday life. Many Psychology courses are accredited and usually courses are governed by the British Psychological Society (BPS). As such, you are required to be professional and committed whilst on a Psychology course. We will therefore cover what you can expect to learn whilst on the course, professionalism, and the importance of taking responsibility for your own learning. Additionally, this chapter hopes to get you thinking about why you want to study Psychology, and what has impacted on your decision to embark on your journey.

Overview of topics

- What is Psychology and who are Psychologists?
- How can Psychology be used in everyday life?
- How can Psychology be used in practice?
- What will I learn during my degree?
- What are the expectations of Psychology students?

> ### Learning outcomes
> 1 To better understand what Psychology is, how it can be used in everyday life, and how we can apply it in practice
> 2 To identify what is expected of you as a Psychology student
> 3 To identify what you can expect to learn while you study for your Psychology degree

What is Psychology and who are Psychologists?

Where do we begin? Psychology is so vast and varied, it would be impossible to cover everything here, but we will dispel a few myths! First and foremost, those who study Psychology cannot read people's minds, nor does it qualify them to 'psychoanalyse' others or 'spot a liar'. In reality, Psychology is a scientific study of the mind, with a view to understanding human behaviour. According to the British Psychological Society (2020), Psychology is 'about understanding what makes people tick and how this understanding can help us address many of the problems and issues in society today'. So, overall, Psychology seeks to make sense of human behaviour, and find solutions for real-life problems in society; this could be in many settings and working with various client groups. In Chapter 3 we will discuss what it means to be a Psychologist, and the types of careers you could go into after completing a degree in Psychology, but for now we will cover what a 'Psychologist' is *not*.

Being a Psychologist is often confused with other job roles, so we need to do some myth-busting. Psychologists are *not* Psychiatrists; they are very different job roles, with very different qualifications. Psychiatrists are medically trained doctors, who have then branched into Psychiatry. They can support individuals with mental health issues such as anxiety, psychosis, alcohol/drug addiction, and many more. Psychiatrists can prescribe medicine, Psychologists cannot.

Psychologists are also not therapists. On the television, the terms Psychologist, therapist (or to be more accurate, *Psychotherapist*), and Psychiatrist are often used interchangeably, which can be very confusing! For example, Practising Psychologists, Psychotherapists, and Counsellors can all support individuals to overcome stress as well as a range of other problems (e.g. depression, anxiety, difficulties in relationships, managing emotions such as aggression). However, in order to practise therapy as a Psychologist, you would need to complete a doctorate programme in Clinical or Counselling Psychology (more on this in Chapter 3). Psychotherapists tend to specialise in one mode of therapy (e.g. psychodynamic therapy) and have extensive training on this specific therapeutic model. Counsellors may also focus on one particular model of therapy but will be trained exclusively on the development of practical counselling skills.

The terms Psychotherapist and Counsellor are also often used interchangeably. Counsellors are individuals who have been specifically trained in counselling to support individuals with psychological problems; they will also be a member of the British Association for Counselling and Psychotherapy (BACP). You may be the person your friends go to when they want to talk about their problems, but this does not make you a Counsellor; you may however have the skills needed to be one (www.bacp.co.uk).

How can Psychology be used in everyday life?

Psychology is everywhere, and can be applied in many situations. During the course of your Psychology degree you will learn about several theories, and you will get to know the research around various topics. You will become well acquainted with reading! But your family and friends might initially ask, 'Why study Psychology? What is it?', so to help you explain, here are some examples of Psychology in everyday life.

To start us off, there are the simple principles of Behavioural Psychology. For example, in training your pet, you reward good behaviour, which encourages them to repeat it. Some parents also do this with children, e.g. giving them 'gold stars' for good behaviour. As we said before, Psychology is about 'what makes people tick', so as Psychologists we seek to understand others' behaviours, including problem behaviours (e.g. bullying in schools) and good behaviours (e.g. children being kind to one another). You might see this as common sense, but it is Psychology!

Other examples of Psychology in everyday life include social behaviours. You will have noticed that people behave in specific ways in various situations. For example, a friend may experience peer pressure to drink alcohol in a bar or pub. Or when working in a group, you may notice one person 'social loafing', where they let others do the work. These examples are explained using principles of Social Psychology.

Also, during periods of stress, such as exams, people will respond in different ways. These include alcohol or substance abuse, developing a physical illness, displaying a mental illness (e.g. anxiety disorders), or using principles of resilience. The ways in which people react to stress will depend on various factors, such as their personality, environment, genetics, or available coping strategies. All of this is Psychology in action!

While Psychologists are not mind readers (despite many, many, many people asking you to 'read their minds' as soon as they find out you're studying Psychology), what psychological knowledge does support you in is being able to better understand behavioural changes in those around you. For example, if a family member is experiencing depression, you may notice signs that their behaviour has changed. Armed with this psychological knowledge, you will be able to identify these indicators and changes. You may also be able to better help them to seek support from a professional.

As you may know already, everyone has different preferences when it comes to learning. Psychology can help individuals understand about their own (and others') learning preferences, and to apply techniques to support people to retain information. Psychology also helps us explore concepts of intelligence, and tools have been developed (because of Psychology) to help us understand more about learning difficulties.

So overall, Psychology has a huge impact on everyday life. Just as importantly, Psychology has been developed to support individuals in practice settings.

How can Psychology be used in practice?

As we keep saying, Psychology is huge and it is everywhere! There are many different types of Psychologist, in many settings (covered in more detail in Chapter 3). Here we will give some examples of how Psychology can be applied in practice to support individuals or groups of people.

In forensic settings (e.g. working with prisoners, ex-offenders, and/or victims), it is important that professionals who work with people who have committed an offence are aware of each individual's areas of risk to themselves and others, and what protective factors the individual may have (i.e. things that will potentially stop them from offending). Thus, Forensic Psychologists have sought to develop 'risk assessments' that can be used as a tool to 'predict' the likelihood of future behaviours, such as the risk of future violence, sexual offences, or Intimate Partner Violence (IPV). Forensic Psychologists use these risk assessment tools to gain an idea of what situations or factors may trigger particular behaviours, and what protective factors can be drawn on to help prevent such behaviours. By understanding areas of risk and protective factors for individuals, Forensic Psychologists can develop treatment programmes which work on areas of risk and encourage them to apply their protective factors.

In clinical settings (e.g. health centres, hospitals, private practice), Clinical Psychologists may be asked to help identify psychological, behavioural, or emotional issues and work with service users to develop a suitable intervention/treatment plan based on relevant theory and evidence-based research; they are responsible for monitoring the progress of their clients through regular meetings. Clinical Psychologists often report the results of research studies to test the effectiveness of certain types of Psychotherapy in published journals. These are just a few examples of the many tasks that Clinical Psychologists engage with on a day-to-day basis.

In schools, Educational Psychologists may be called upon to support a child with their learning and development. For example, a teacher may have observed that a child has difficulties with their reading. An Educational Psychologist might then decide to carry out some tests to examine possible deficits in language processing, such as dyslexia. Once the Psychologist has an idea as to the child's areas of strength and development, they can work with the teachers and parents to put support in place.

Hopefully by now you can see that Psychology is useful in many practical situations. Depending on the Psychology degree you pursue (some degrees focus on a particular element of Psychology such as Forensic or Sport), you will learn about how Psychology is applied, theories in Psychology, statistics, and, in your final year, you will have the opportunity to contribute towards Psychological knowledge with your own independent research project. This might lead you to question what else you'll be learning, so let's take a look.

What will I learn during my degree?

Psychology is one of the most popular subjects to study at degree level. According to the Quality Assurance Agency (QAA), 'A third of graduates who go into permanent employment as Psychologists enter public services (such as the health service, education, the civil service, and the armed forces), and a third go into industry or commerce, for example market research and personnel management' (QAA, 2019, p. 3). This shows that your learning can be applied in many different types of workplace.

If you wish to pursue a career in Psychology, you will be required to have Graduate Basis for Chartership (GBC), which you can obtain by successfully achieving a 2:1 or above on an accredited degree course. Most Psychology degrees are accredited by the British Psychological Society (we will look at the BPS in more depth in Chapter 3), and there are certain things you will need to learn in order to meet the QAA benchmark competencies for your degree. Psychology degree courses are required to teach psychological theories and how they can be applied to real-life settings, as well as ethics, and cultural and individual differences. It is likely your University will cover the following branches (BPS, 2019):

- Biological Psychology
- Cognitive Psychology
- Social Psychology
- Developmental Psychology
- Individual differences
- Conceptual and historical issues in Psychology
- Research methods

Accredited Psychology qualifications must cover a core set of curriculum topics, so there will be overlap between institutions. However, you may find individual module titles differ and/or how a topic is taught. It is also important to note that core areas are subject to change; specifically, if the British Psychological Society updates its guides and standards, institutions must do the same. This helps ensure your degree is current and relevant.

One important thing to remember is that there will be certain aspects of Psychology that interest you, and those that don't, which is perfectly okay – but you still need to have a broad understanding of the discipline as a whole. Skipping classes because they are 'boring' or 'I'll never need that information' is a poor attitude. Knowledge is power!

As per the QAA competencies, you are required to develop subject-specific competencies, i.e. skills that relate to Psychology. Some examples include: applying theory to psychological issues, generating and testing hypotheses utilising theories, carrying out empirical studies using a variety of methods (both qualitative and quantitative; see Chapter 6 for the differences), employing evidence-based reasoning, using specialist software (e.g. SPSS), critically evaluating theory and research, and showing an awareness of ethical issues. This list is not exhaustive so if you want to read more about the subject-specific standards, access www.qaa.ac.uk. It is important to remember that you won't know absolutely everything about Psychology by the end of your degree. You may have found a topic you really like and develop knowledge around that, for your dissertation for example, but even then there will be much more to learn. Psychology for most is a lifelong mission, and the learning never stops. Continue to be curious and read, read, read!

The QAA requires that you also develop generic skills. Some of these skills include: effective communication (written and verbal), numerical reasoning skills, being computer literate (e.g. competence in using Microsoft Word), retrieving and organising information effectively, recognising the skills needed for effective teamwork, and taking responsibility for your own learning. You will be supported to develop these skills throughout your degree, but you can also undertake additional activities such as work experience (which show you are taking responsibility and wanting to develop professionally and personally). There will also be practical modules that will help you develop as a Psychologist. Such modules are important to help you develop skills such as interviewing, identifying your strengths and limitations, help with time management, reflection, and being able to articulate your own transferable and employability skills. So, we really recommend that you engage with those modules; they may not be the jazziest modules, but they will be the most important in supporting you in your career development.

Overall, Psychology degrees are designed to provide you with knowledge of some of the theories in Psychology, research methods, and the skills to work in the field. A Psychology degree does not bestow on you the title of 'Psychologist', but you will certainly be heading in the right direction towards a career in Psychology. Equally, your degree may give you insight into other career options; even if you decide you don't want to be a Psychologist, your Psychology degree will prepare you for lots of other career choices if you embrace it. You won't be a mind reader or be able to 'spot a liar' by the end of your degree … not ever in fact! But you will be well prepared and have the skills to be a valued employee no matter what career you decide to pursue.

What are the expectations of Psychology students?

As we keep saying, Psychology degrees are *professional courses*, which means that from the very start, whether you are at the University or at home on social media, you should adhere to the BPS code of conduct for students (we cover this in more depth in Chapter 3).

As academics, we have our own expectations of you too. At degree level we expect that you will be independent learners. This does not mean you can't ask for help, but rather you should try to seek the answers to the questions you have with the information available. If you are unable to find the answer then, of course, seek the appropriate help. It is not, for example, appropriate to email lecturers asking them for information that is likely already available on your learning platforms (e.g. Moodle, Aula, Canvas, Blackboard), such as assignment deadlines. It would, however, be acceptable to approach academic staff if you wanted to discuss, for example, an idea for your dissertation.

At degree level, we have an expectation that you will take responsibility for your own learning. This includes reading any recommended resources given to you (and finding your own resources), completing in-session and out-of-session tasks, managing your time appropriately so that you are not late handing work in, and accessing support services (e.g. career services, support with academic writing). Also, we highly recommend you further build on your skills by engaging with volunteering, paid work, work experience, or placements.

While we don't expect you to know exactly what you want to do straight away, it is important to start to think about what interests you, what types of career you might consider, and begin to construct your career development journey. As such, we expect that you will do the appropriate 'groundwork' so that you have a rough idea as to which direction you are heading in, and what you need to do to get there. We discuss career pathways in Chapter 3.

Other things to remember include:

1   Write professional emails to staff, being mindful that an email is a professional communication and is not WhatsApp or Facebook chat (see Figures 2.1 and 2.2 below for examples of how to write and how not to write an email; also see Chapter 4 on professionalism for more information).

2   Turn up to classes on time.

3   Whilst in class be respectful of others – for example, don't talk over others, put your mobile phone away and on silent, and don't misuse learning tools (e.g. don't write offensive words or intrusive questions about staff or other students).

4   Don't turn up at the office of a member of academic staff – or try to call them or engage in online meetings – unannounced.

5   Always give staff ample time for a meeting. It is absolutely not acceptable to email a member of staff the evening before you want to meet with them, or expect a response to an email on a Sunday morning that you sent on Saturday evening (despite popular belief, we do have social lives you know!).

6   Staff generally have an agreed response turnaround time (depending on the institution), so email in advance and do not expect a response straightaway.

7   Be mindful that staff will have a number of duties to carry out; they will get back to you at some point, so patience is key.

8   Make sure you email the right person with your question. For example, your personal tutor (or equivalent) is unlikely to know your assessment deadline; you will need to ask your module leader that ... or even better, check your learning platforms first, as you will likely find it there!

9   Always ask staff if they are happy to be your referee before putting their name down. Due to Data Protection legislation they will be unable to provide a reference without your permission, and have every right not to provide a reference if they have not been asked politely.

10 Do not slate your University, academic staff, or other students on social media and learning platforms. This includes receiving a grade that was lower than expected and then posting a message such as 'has anyone else been marked by [name]?' whilst including clown emojis. This is not professional! And imagine how you would feel if someone did the same to you. If you have a genuine complaint, there will be ways and means of addressing it in an appropriate (and professional) way.

You will have been given a shedload of information in your induction. This can feel overwhelming, and you will likely have forgotten a lot of it. So, if in doubt about who to contact, check your induction paperwork or any community pages you're enrolled on before emailing staff. The information is usually somewhere, and staff won't be impressed when asked questions you can easily find the answer to yourself, or they know they have answered already (see Table 2.1).

Table 2.1 Who to ask

Question/query	Staff member
Course-related questions, e.g. I would like to swap courses and I need someone to sign the paperwork	The course director (your institution may use a different term). Who this is should be displayed on your learning platform (e.g. Moodle, Aula, Canvas, or Blackboard) or in any induction paperwork you may have. If you are unsure you could always ask a member of staff you know well who might be able to point you in the right direction
Module-related questions, i.e. any queries you may have about the module or assignment (if the information is not already available)	The module leader. Who this is, is usually displayed on your learning platform for each module. Make sure you get the right person to avoid time wasting and confusion
Questions relating to careers	You could discuss your career options and your future with your personal tutor (or equivalent title). They may point you towards the careers team at your University too. But please note they can only advise, they cannot tell you exactly what to do or which career would best suit you; that's for you to decide. You know you best!
Pastoral care, e.g. I'm struggling with my studies and need support	Again, you can approach your personal tutor (or equivalent title) to discuss why you might be struggling. They will be able to advise who to ask for specific help. For example, it might be practical support you need such as help with academic writing, or they might suggest you speak with the University Counselling Service
Extensions or deferrals	You can discuss this with your personal tutor (or equivalent title), however they are likely to refer you to your University registry team as they are the best people to advise you

(continued)

Table 2.1   (continued)

Question/query	Staff member
Complaints about grades	In most institutions you cannot appeal your grade based on academic judgement. However, if you feel there were extenuating circumstances that impacted on your ability to achieve a decent grade, you must go through the appropriate channels. This will likely be through the University's registry department; they should be able to point you in the right direction
Feedback from your assignment	Usually, the best person to approach is your marker. They marked your work, so they are best placed to tell you!

Figure 2.1 Screenshot of an unprofessional email

Take a look at the screenshot of the email in Figure 2.1. Here the subject is blank, so the staff member can't possibly know what the email is about – we're not psychic you know! There is also an inappropriate salutation ('Heya'), although sometimes there is no salutation at all – no 'dear' or 'hello', but there was once an 'Oi'! In addition, the student has not stated what they want to meet the staff member about or when – again we are not mind readers and how could we possibly assess the urgency of this request? Furthermore, the student has signed off inappropriately; instead of 'Jenz', we would expect to see the student's full name and student number. Remember, emails are professional means of communication and are not like instant messaging such as on WhatsApp or Facebook Messenger – so please don't 'LOL' us! And don't send us several emails in quick succession. We get lots of emails every day, so there is a chance we might miss something if

Figure 2.2 Screenshot of a professional email

To	staff member		Bcc
Cc			

Meeting to discuss assignment feedback

Dear John,

I hope you are well.

As the marker of my assignment, I am writing to ask if you are available the week commencing 15th November to discuss my feedback for 5000PY (the developing as a Psychologist module)?

I look forward to hearing from you

Best wishes,
Jenny Anderson
7675739

we receive more than one email from you, plus it comes across as though you haven't taken the time to think about what it is you really want to say.

Now take a look at the screenshot in Figure 2.2, where we have an appropriate salutation. Moreover, the focus is very clear: the student is asking for something specific (i.e. feedback) in relation to a specific module. In our experience, students often fail to include the module code so it is good practice to include this information as well as a clear purpose for contacting the staff member. And this time 'Jenz' has signed off appropriately!

Activity 2.1: Reflecting on why I am doing this course

Now you know what Psychology is, how it can be applied in everyday life and practice, what you will learn during your degree, and staff expectations of students, it is time for you to take a moment or two to think about why you want to study Psychology. Once you have done so, make some notes in the box below about the following: Why do I want to study Psychology? What strengths do I have that might help me with my degree? What may I need to work on? What biases do I have about certain areas of Psychology? (For example, lots of people say they wouldn't want to work with sex offenders.) What experiences, if any, have influenced my choice of course/career?

Activity 2.2: Discuss at least three expectations tutors will have of you as a Psychology student:

Chapter resources

For the **QAA benchmark competencies** for your degree, see: https://www.qaa.ac.uk/docs/qaa/subject-benchmark-statements/subject-benchmark-statement-psychology.pdf?sfvrsn=6935c881_13

References

British Psychological Society (BPS) (2019). *Standards for the accreditation of undergraduate, conversion and integrated Masters programmes in psychology*. https://www.bps.org.uk/sites/bps.org.uk/files/Accreditation/Undergraduate%20Accreditation%20Handbook%202019.pdf

British Psychological Society (BPS) (2020). *About us*. https://www.bps.org.uk/public/what-is-psychology

Quality Assurance Agency for UK Higher Education (QAA) (2019). *The Subject Benchmark Statement for Psychology*. https://www.qaa.ac.uk/docs/qaa/subject-benchmark-statements/subject-benchmark-statement-psychology.pdf?sfvrsn=6935c881_13

Activity 2.1: Example answer

There are no correct answers! What you write will depend on your individual aims, skillset, and expectations. Answering the questions will help you get thinking about this.

Activity 2.2: Example answer

There are a number of things you could discuss here, such as adhering to the BPS Code of Conduct at all times, including being respectful of others, recognising your own competence, being responsible, and having integrity. You could also talk about how important it is to be an independent learner (e.g. seeking out information for yourself but taking the initiative to ask for help when appropriate) and taking responsibility for your own learning (e.g. engaging with recommended reading, managing your time, and accessing support services when necessary). You could also talk about the importance of appropriate emails, turning up to sessions and meetings on time, and acting appropriately on social media (including refraining from slating the University, staff, and other students). This list is not exhaustive but offers you some examples of what expectations staff will have of you.

3 The British Psychological Society and career pathways

Psychology degrees are managed by the British Psychological Society (BPS). So, we will introduce who the BPS are and why they are important. For those of you interested in Chartership, we'll also introduce you to the Health and Care Professions Council (HCPC) briefly covering who they are and what it means to be 'Chartered'. Additionally, we will outline how the BPS expects students to behave, discuss the topic umbrellas in Psychology, and provide some example career pathways (including some for if you decide a career in Psychology is not for you!).

Overview of topics

- Who are the BPS? What is HCPC? And why are they important?
- Should I be behaving in accordance with the BPS now?
- What is a Psychologist? And what does it mean to be Chartered?
- Example career pathways
- What happens if I decide Psychology isn't for me?

Learning outcomes

1 To gain an understanding of who the BPS and HCPC are and why they are important
2 To develop awareness of expectations the BPS has for student behaviour
3 To explore the various 'umbrellas' in Psychology and to see example career pathways
4 To learn more about what happens if someone decides Psychology is not for them

Who are the BPS? What is the HCPC? And why are they important?

The British Psychological Society (BPS) is 'a registered charity which acts as the representative body for Psychology and Psychologists in the UK, and is responsible for the promotion of excellence and ethical practice in the science, education, and application of the discipline' (BPS, 2020). Their aim is to ensure standards in Psychology (e.g. students, academics and practitioners, research, education, and practice/application) are all of a high standard. Students can become registered members of the BPS when they start their course, and then become graduate members upon successful completion of their degree. For the most up-to-date information on the BPS, go to the BPS website (www.bps.org.uk).

The Health Care and Professions Council (HCPC) sets standards for professionals, including Chartered Psychologists. Psychologists who have been successful in their traineeship and wish to become Chartered will be required to register with the HCPC. The HCPC have several expectations of their registrants, including standards for their training, professional skills, behaviour, and health. These standards cover education (e.g. how degrees are managed and delivered), the conduct and performance of practising professionals (e.g. not practising outside your area of expertise), and proficiency (e.g. fitness to practise, good professional judgement). They also emphasise continuing professional development (ah, you can never escape the push to be a lifelong learner!!) to ensure knowledge and skillsets are kept up to date.

The HCPC are dynamic and responsive and will develop standards when circumstances arise, such as during the Covid-19 pandemic. To learn more about the HCPC, go to the HCPC website (www.hcpc-uk.org).

So, why are the BPS and HCPC important? Well, in short, they set the standards for you as a student, for academic staff, and for practitioners. They are there to ensure that we are all acting ethically, treating others with dignity and respect, working within our competence, and developing ourselves. This latter point is key because even when you have completed your degree (and Charter as a Psychologist), you will still have areas that need developing and/or new knowledge will become available. We should all strive to be lifelong learners and, as Psychologists, it is important to be guided by professional standards to continue to develop our skillset. So, remember, when you complete your degree you will have gained lots of skills, but there will still be room for development (even when you are 15–20 years into your career you'll find there are still things to learn!!). We will look at the importance of reflecting on your strengths and limitations, plus digesting feedback, in Chapter 5. There we will explain why reflection and learning from feedback are important for your career development. Following the principles set out by the BPS and HCPC, however, will always be an essential part of being a Psychologist.

Should I be behaving in accordance with the BPS now?

Yes! BPS accredited Psychology degrees are *professional courses*. This means that, from the very start, whether you are at the University completing your assignments, or at home on social media, you should adhere to the BPS Code of Conduct. This Code contains four ethical principles:

1 **Respect** – for the dignity of others
2 **Competence** – recognising strengths and limitations and acting within your abilities
3 **Responsibility** – ensuring the trust of others is not exploited, there is no abuse of power, and that duty towards others is paramount
4 **Integrity** – being honest, accurate, and fair (BPS, 2018)

You can look at the BPS Code of Conduct in more depth on the BPS website (www.bps.org.uk), and also in Chapter 4 of this book. But broadly speaking, you are required to uphold high standards of professionalism, ethical behaviour, and good judgement. You will quickly learn that in Psychology we are constantly faced with ethical decisions, starting with your time at University – whether that be a friend asking to copy your work, or a participant revealing to you during an interview that they have committed an offence. So, it is important that you start behaving in an ethical and professional manner from the outset. The BPS student guide supports you in making ethical decisions and highlights the importance of professionalism. Thus, if you are ever unsure about your conduct, or need support in responding to a tricky situation, you may want to refer back to the BPS Code of Conduct or speak to a trusted tutor.

What is a Psychologist? And what does it mean to be Chartered?

So far, we have mentioned Chartership quite a lot. You might be thinking, 'What does it mean to be Chartered?' and 'How do I get there?' We'll cover the basics here, but you may wish to research your chosen area in more depth, since different types of Psychologist will likely follow different, or multiple, routes to becoming Chartered. Also, the routes to Chartership can change, which is why we recommend you consult the BPS for the most up-to-date information.

Chartered (practising) 'Psychologist' is a protected title. This is earned through intense study and practical work experience; you won't become a Chartered Psychologist after completing your Bachelor of Science degree, but it is certainly a step in the right direction if you do want to become a Chartered (and practising) Psychologist. You can also become a Chartered Psychologist through research, where practice experience is not essential.

Psychologists work in various settings, including: clinical settings (e.g. hospitals, health centres, social services, private practice), forensic settings (e.g. prisons, probation, in the community), education/with children, the workplace, health settings, the military, and the sporting industry. It would be impossible to list all of the duties of a Psychologist, as these vary depending on the field they work in, but in general the following are the types of Psychologist practising in the UK today:

- Clinical
- Forensic
- Business
- Occupational
- Sport
- Educational
- Counselling
- Health
- Neurological

For more information on careers in Psychology, see: www.careers.bps.org.uk.

Below we highlight the career pathways of the three authors, to show that there are many options for you to pursue after your degree – and quite often your path changes!

Example career pathways

Amy's career timeline

Figure 3.1 shows Amy's career timeline. This shows you how her career has progressed over time, starting with her undergraduate and postgraduate degrees. Different patterns denote different types of roles under the career path. You will see that there have been several occasions when an external factor (denoted by the ✳ symbol) influenced her decision-making. The first is an example of a setback considered in Chapter 5 when someone refused to send her an application form for a job she wanted to apply for. This post was totally different to the research role she eventually landed.

Figure 3.1 Amy's career timeline

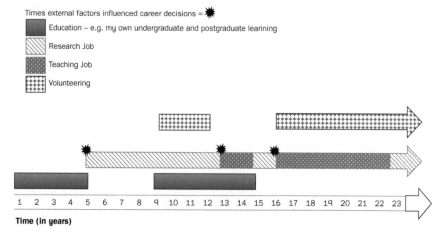

The second 'crisis' was being made redundant during a recession when Amy had to determine how she could keep earning whilst completing her PhD part-time. This led to what amounted to a side-step in her plans, as she took a role as a Training Coordinator for a security company. You'll see that she moved back into research once her PhD was completed but again took another side-step when her father fell ill and she needed more job security to help care for him. This culminated in a long diversion into teaching at Universities whilst she supported her family. Once stable, she was able to consider moving back to research again.

This example career path is a useful way to think about how external factors play a role in our decision-making. Amy ended up in roles she had not previously considered. She learned a lot and met a lot of great people. Working (and succeeding) in different roles can also help you identify what you do (and do not!) want to make a career out of.

Daniel's career timeline

Figure 3.2 shows Daniel's career timeline. Once Daniel completed his second master's degree, he did some training to obtain experience which could contribute towards a DClinPsy application. Daniel applied through clearing, but was rejected for the doctorate course he hoped to get onto. Shortly afterwards, his partner received an offer to study for a three-year degree at University. This was a critical moment – Daniel re-evaluated his abilities and career plan, and chose to study instead for a PhD. Alongside his PhD, he also began teaching as part of the studentship, which provided valuable experience. At the end of the studentship, however, there were limited opportunities for him to teach, and his PhD still needed to be written up and completed, so Daniel returned to training.

Figure 3.2 Daniel's career timeline

Times external factors influenced career decsions = ✳

Education – e.g. my own undergraduate and postgraduate learning

Research Job

Teaching Job

Practitioner Job

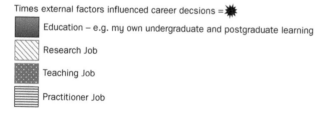
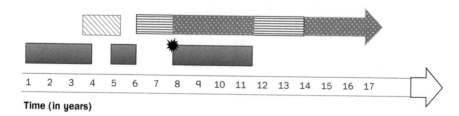

Time (in years)

Throughout his career journey, Daniel's main skill and interest was in conducting and analysing research, but he was focused too much on the need to gain relevant experience for the DClinPsy. Daniel realised he was excited about not only conducting research, but also teaching research methods, so waited for the right opportunity to come along (whilst still writing articles for publication and being an active researcher).

As you can see, Daniels's has been a very different career pathway – he was uncertain about what type of Psychologist he wanted to be (or should be): practitioner or academic. Having a meeting with a career advisor focusing on strengths would certainly have been useful, although the experience gained from his training has helped broaden Daniel's awareness of clinical behaviours, which continues to inform his teaching!

Rachael's career timeline

Figure 3.3 show's Rachael's career timeline. Before going to University Rachael took a year out to work, completing an NVQ in Business Administration (working in a credit union). It was during this time that Rachael had the chance to reflect on her career options, and ultimately chose to study for a degree in Psychology with Counselling. After graduating, she embarked on and completed a master's in Forensic Psychology. Whilst studying, she volunteered at Headway West Midlands (working with individuals with acquired brain injury) and Supporting Others Through Voluntary Action (SOVA; working with both adult and youth ex-offenders) and was ultimately offered paid positions in both companies.

Figure 3.3 Rachael's career timeline

Times external factors influenced career decsions = ✳

Education – e.g. my own undergraduate and postgraduate learining

Research Job

Teaching Job

Practitioner Job

Volunteering

1 2 3 4 5 6 7 8 9 10 11 12 13 14

Time (in years)

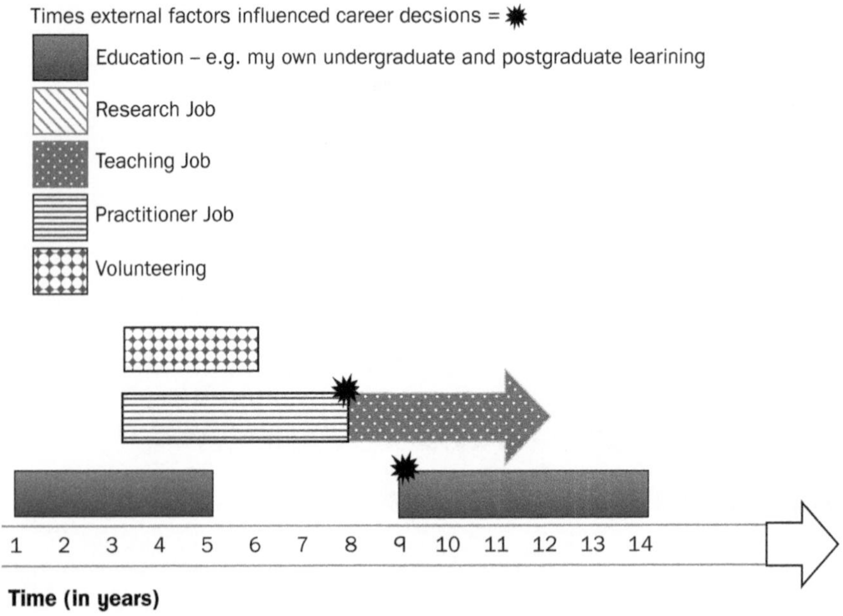

After completing her studies, she worked for the prison system delivering accredited programmes to male sex offenders, and began guest speaking at Coventry University. It was at this point Rachael decided to make a career change. At first, she was not successful in applying for a lectureship, but after gaining further experience in management at the prison, she re-applied and secured a permanent lecturer post. Yet Rachael faced one further hurdle: whilst lecturing, she applied to the PhD programme but was unable to start until she had completed her Postgraduate Certificate in Higher Education.

What happens if I decide Psychology isn't for me?

First, don't panic! You might be feeling as though you have wasted your time or feel a little lost. It's normal to feel like that! But you have not wasted your time, and you won't feel lost forever. You might want to look back through Chapter 2 (what will I learn in my degree, specifically the skills relating to the QAA) to identify what skills you have developed during your degree; this might help you think about what you enjoyed doing and what you didn't enjoy so much. Once you've thought about what interests you, and what your strengths are, this will help you start to think about what your next move is. Remember, you are not alone. Speak to your University's career services, speak to your tutors and other students, and do your research on potential career pathways! You will spend a lot of time at work, so you will want to make the right career choice. If you are open minded to different options you may fall into something you really enjoy, or even turn a hobby into a career.

Other options open to you after your degree that relate to Psychology but are not necessarily Chartership-focused include: further training (e.g. on the job as a probation officer, therapy training, teacher training) or a master's degree, support work (with various types of clients, e.g. brain injury, learning difficulties, autism), Assistant Psychologist roles, market research (or research in general if it interests you), teaching assistant roles, and healthcare work.

You may think, 'I don't want to be a Psychologist and have zero interest in Psychology-related job roles at all'. And that's fine too. You will have learned lots of generic skills, including: computer literacy, communicating appropriately with different audiences, organising information effectively, and working as part of a team. This makes you a great candidate for lots of jobs unrelated to Psychology. There are so many jobs out there! So, the best advice we can give you is to spend some time looking at job sites, seeing what's out there (and what the requirements are), and speak to your family, friends, other students, and the career service at your University. There is a job out there that is perfect for you, but be prepared to have to work towards it by doing additional work experience or extra training. What's important is that you map out what your perfect career is, what you need to do to get there, and set yourself some goals. As highlighted above in the 'example career pathways', everyone's journey is different, but it is a journey nonetheless.

Activity 3.1: Go to the British Psychological Society website and look up the different areas in Psychology (e.g. health, forensic, cognitive) and choose one or two that appeal to you. Make notes about why in the box below.

Activity 3.2: At the end of your course, look at what you wrote down when completing Activity 3.1. Has it changed? If so, why? If not, why not? Again, make notes below.

Chapter resources

For the **BPS website,** see: https://www.bps.org.uk

For the **HCPC website,** see: https://www.hcpc-uk.org

References

British Psychological Society (BPS) (2018). *Code of Ethics and Conduct.* https://www.bps.org.uk/news-and-policy/bps-code-ethics-and-conduct
British Psychological Society (BPS) (2020). *About us.* https://www.bps.org.uk/about-us

Activities 3.1 and 3.2: Example answers

Activities 3.1 and 3.2 were designed to get you thinking about your interests. There are no right answers – just what is right for you!

4 Professionalism

It is essential that students understand that their degree is not separate from their career but an important first step on the ladder. In this chapter we will highlight the importance of professionalism and give you some tips on how to develop the necessary skills. We will cover a range of topics from email etiquette to having an appropriate online presence and many things in between. We hope that this chapter cements your view of Psychology as a professional course, where acting professionally is a key expectation. We will also link back to careers and the opportunities to build and maintain networks whilst still studying. We'll include real-world examples of where students have successfully demonstrated professionalism at University and gained employment as a result. The key message to take away from this chapter is: your journey starts here, so start acting professionally – now!

Overview of topics

- What is professionalism and why is it important?
- How does professionalism link to the BPS?
- Why you should do more than get drunk and party during Freshers (induction) week
- On a professional journey
- Volunteering/work experience
- Practical tips

Learning outcomes

1 To understand why professionalism is expected of you in your undergraduate Psychology course
2 To learn about professionalism in Psychology
3 To have an opportunity to practise your professional skills

---

What is professionalism and why is it important?

Professionalism – like many terms – is bandied about but often without explaining what it means. Stripping this back to its simplest explanation, professionalism means displaying the competence and skills expected of you by your profession. For Psychology, this will include what we would expect of most professionals (e.g. politeness, reliability, delivering to deadlines) but also the competence to practise. As a Psychologist, you will be expected to ensure you uphold professional standards – this ranges from ensuring you complete an appropriately accredited degree and further training (as appropriate) to the development of whatever skills are most relevant to your role. There is also an expectation to engage in ongoing professional development, as your learning doesn't just suddenly come to an end when you graduate. As a Psychologist, you will be expected to keep your skills up to date (as noted in Chapter 3).

However, despite its importance, professionalism is something that is often forgotten and, if managed poorly, can have negative long-term consequences. For instance, imagine you find your dream job and ask your tutor to be a referee. What are they likely to write if you have acted unprofessionally, failed to turn up for class, and/or been rude? Or that you lack competency in key skills?

So, it is imperative that you develop professional skills, right from the very first day of your course. This is not just about being polite and courteous – which, of course, most students are already! – but also how you might adapt your approach to ensure your correspondence with others is more structured and clear, and how you might work to develop the core competence-based skills (more on this in the next section) you will need to become a practising Psychologist.

How does professionalism link to the BPS?

The British Psychological Society (BPS) is the professional body for Psychology and Psychologists in the UK. As such, they have a responsibility for setting and promoting standards for psychological work, including research, education, and practice. There are a whole host of standards and guidelines published by the BPS and it is always a good idea to keep up to date with these. For example:

- Code of Ethics and Conduct: covers such things as informed consent and recruitment of participants – you will need this when conducting your third-year project, so familiarise yourself with it early on!!
- Human Research Ethics: includes how to manage research during difficult times, such as the Covid-19 pandemic.
- Guidelines for working with animals: for example, legal and moral responsibilities, animal welfare.
- Guidance on teaching and assessment in Psychology education: this is what your lecturers should be adhering to!!
- Practice Guidelines: covers legal and professional obligations, reflective practice, working with different types of clients, safeguarding, etc.
- Responsible use of social media: remember, whatever you put on social media stays there. We have all seen examples of people losing their jobs

because of something they said or reposted on social media. Providing details of social media accounts to potential employers is becoming more common, so it is worth thinking about what you post – it could make or break a job application!

Up-to-date standards and guides can be accessed at the BPS website. The BPS also stresses the importance of continuing professional development (CPD), and this is built into many of the guides listed above. For more information on standards and guides and CPD, see the 'resources' section at the end of the chapter.

Another way to boost your knowledge is to join the BPS as a student member. This is the first step into membership of the Society (if you wish to be accredited/go down the Chartered path later, membership of the BPS is essential). There are a range of benefits to membership, including access to events and student online communities as well as discounts and a subscription to their magazines. There is a cost attached to membership but this is discounted for students. Also, ask your tutor or course director (your institution may use different terms) about this – you may find subscriptions to the BPS are available through your course. Again, for more on membership, see the 'resources' section at the end of the chapter.

Why you should do more than get drunk and party during Freshers (induction) week

So, we've already highlighted that you should start acting professionally from day one. This does not mean you have to 'stand on ceremony' at all times and never go out and get drunk and silly with your friends (if that's your bag). However, you should start to separate out your personal and professional life and think about how what you do in your personal life could impact on your career. For example, although you might have one too many with your mates in a social context, you ought to think more carefully about your alcohol consumption when in a professional space – think of the horror stories you hear about office Christmas parties and you'll get an idea of what you need to avoid! It's not unheard of for people who drank too much at a work event to lose their job over it. In one case, someone called the head of Human Resources at their company a very rude word (which we won't repeat here) and found their P45 in the post the next day. Although this is an extreme example (and nothing to do with Psychology we hasten to add!), you can see how behaving unprofessionally can have disastrous consequences.

There will be lots of opportunities for you to display your professionalism from the outset. First of all, attend induction sessions – these outline key information about your course and, even if you don't need the information straight-away, you can always come back to it later. For example, although you might think the session on the library will be dull, just think about your first assignment: your notes from a session on the library will be indispensable when locating the books/resources you need for your topic, trying to book quiet a space to work, or searching the library catalogue effectively – in short, this information will become very useful very quickly! Induction is also an opportunity to start getting to know staff on the course, some of whom you might not be taught by straightaway. Going to induction means you get to know who is on the team and what their specialist topics are, which can be useful later, especially when coming up with ideas for your dissertation. Many tutors are happy to meet with students to talk about careers, so you can start looking at booking a slot during staff office hours to find out more about options (e.g. what kind of experience is useful for a job you are interested in post-graduation, or the pros and cons of different career choices). We have ex-police officers and people who have worked in prisons in our Forensic Psychology team, for example – many students don't realise this, as they don't make the effort to get to know staff outside of the classroom. What an untapped resource!

Similarly, get to know your seminar tutors – just because they are teaching you one topic doesn't mean that is all they know about. Take the time to have a chat with them to see what extra nuggets of information you can pick up. We would also encourage you to get to know your peers, many of whom will work in related fields and you will find you can learn from their experiences too.

Induction sessions (and early classes) will likely involve icebreaker activities. As cringeworthy as these might seem (we hated them too when we were students!), they are a great way to start to open up conversations and get to know staff and other students. You will start to build a social network, which can also help to develop your professional network. Many students we have taught who have graduated and now do interesting jobs stay in touch. In fact, some even come back as guest speakers or tutors on the courses they used to attend!

In short, we encourage you to see all sessions and activities as an opportunity to get to know others and learn. This will stand you in good stead.

On a professional journey

One of the best ways to think about your career in Psychology is that you are on a professional journey and University is the first step. There are lots of things you can do to help support your journey. For example:

- Turn up to class: if you snooze, you lose! You might have the slides but that's not the same as being in a class (face-to-face or online) hearing someone explain content to you.
- Be on time: pretty obvious really but this is not just about your learning (which you will get more of if you are on time) – being on time also means you don't disrupt others as you try to find your seat. If you are late (and we appreciate this does happen sometimes) try to be as quiet as possible and sit in the first available seat you find (or on the end of a row if you need to come

down towards the front). And a brief apology and explanation to the tutor at the end of the class is always appreciated as well!

- Try not to leave half-way through a lecture/seminar/workshop without good reason, such as 'you can't be bothered'. If you do have to leave, wait for a break and let the tutor know you're leaving. If of course you are genuinely poorly or have an emergency, your tutor will understand.

- Use technology appropriately: follow your tutor's instructions about the use of technology in class. Sometimes personal devices are needed – but when they are not, switch them off or put on silent, and put them away so you are not distracted.

- Pay attention: there is no point being there if you don't listen. Take notes if this is your preference.

- Take part in activities: don't be shy, taking part in activities really enhances your learning experience, especially in small seminar/workshop classes where the emphasis is likely to be on activity-based learning. Remember your tutor is not trying to catch you out – they are trying to engage you in learning!

- Ask questions: if you are unsure, ask. This is important to ensure you understand core topics. You don't need to do this in front of other people. If you would rather, ask at the end of the class or use whatever Q&A mechanism has been set up by your tutor. This is especially important for assessment, as you need to ensure you understand what you need to do.

- Talk to guest speakers: if an external speaker comes to give a talk on your course, take the opportunity to ask them questions. This will further expand your knowledge and help you continue to build a professional network.

- Be sensitive to other students' experiences: Psychology includes a range of difficult and/or controversial topics. Please be mindful of others in your discussions of these, especially things like crime, eating disorders, and bullying. Your peers might have had negative life experiences that could surface as they discuss these issues. You should also remember that people may have different perspectives or views to you (whether religious, cultural, or LGBTQIA+, for example) and there should be space for everyone to be heard.

- Have an appropriate online presence: if you have a professional network page (such as LinkedIn), it should be relatively easy to keep professional. However, be mindful of what you post on other social media sites. The internet is forever.

- Be aware of academic integrity (see Chapter 8 for more information).

- Do the reading: not just the set textbooks but also the module guide/curriculum and assessment information. We have each lost count of the times we are asked basic questions that are clearly addressed in the module materials. Staff are not Google and are not there at your behest to answer a million questions you can easily answer for yourself – so, do the reading! It might be easier for you to ask staff but it does not demonstrate the level of independence that we would expect of students. Whilst we encourage questions for scholarly enquiry, interest, or clarification, don't be surprised if your tutor takes a deep sigh if you ask what the word count is for the essay you are about to submit.

• Think about non-course events: attend talks, lectures, or events that are not part of your course but might be interesting. These can expand your mind and knowledge as well as your professional network.

Remember, professionalism is not just how you behave in the classroom. As the above list shows, it also involves how seriously you take your studies and how you portray yourself externally (e.g. on social media). You are a representative of your University and anything you do that could bring the University into disrepute could have serious consequences. You don't want to lose your place at University because you make an ill-advised / rude / inappropriate comment on social media!!

Professionalism also extends to how you interact with tutors and other staff. Be courteous to support staff (e.g. Registry, IT, and cleaning staff) as well as to teaching staff. All University staff work hard and your University experience wouldn't be possible without all these people, so please do remember that when talking to them. We appreciate that there will be times when you are frustrated – you can't get your laptop to work or you can't see a grade – but you should maintain your professional approach at all times. Not only is this polite, it is also expected.

One way to think about it is to treat others as you would expect to be treated yourself. Take, for example, our experience of being asked for a reference by a student who fails to turn up for one-to-one meetings without explanation or, when they do, they are late and unprepared. Students sometimes think this doesn't matter because we, as their tutors, are being paid. But that's not the point – that slot could have been devoted to seeing another student instead of being wasted; or we could have been doing something else constructive. Imagine if you arrived early for a class only to find the tutor couldn't be bothered to arrive on time; or that they moved the class without telling you beforehand? How would you feel? Would that be professional? Of course not! We know that most students would not dream of behaving this way but some do and you do not want to be the student your tutor remembers for all the wrong reasons!!

Volunteering/work experience

One way to cultivate your professionalism is to start talking to professionals outside the University. Volunteering and/or work experience is one way to do this. It provides you with an opportunity to build networks of people who share your professional interests as well as practise key skills (such as time-keeping, time management, problem-solving, etc.). A good impression here might lead to job opportunities further down the line. We have had several students who have done work experience in a police department before graduating and are now working there full-time, partly because they performed well and behaved professionally throughout their work experience. On the flip side, we also know students who have done the opposite and been fired. For example, one student had an Assistant Psychologist placement, but spent all their time in the office reading case notes rather than being proactive shadowing staff and taking on responsibilities. Moreover, this student was often late for their shift and left early. Not only does this reflect badly on the individual student but also the University. So much so that an employer might not provide the same opportunity the following year, depriving future students of the chance to do work experience with that employer.

Practical tips

We've covered a lot in this chapter but there are a few more points we would like to make. Here goes:

- Email etiquette – always draft emails appropriately. By this we mean using 'Dear ...' and making sure your message is clear (e.g. if you are asking about an assessment, ensure you tell the person which module you are referring to). Be polite and end with your name and student number. Always put something in the subject line. Do not flag your request (🚩) unless it is urgent – and by this we mean actually urgent rather than you wanting a quick answer. See Chapter 2 for an example of good and not so good email structures.

- Class etiquette – we addressed this above but it is useful to summarise. Remember that your learning experience is only as good as the environment you and your peers help create. If you are messing around at the back, you won't learn anything. Similarly, if others are being disruptive you might become distracted, making your learning difficult. If you are experiencing anything like this, report it to your tutor (they can't always see who is doing what and will appreciate some intelligence on this!). Also, and sorry if you think we sound like a broken record, but mobile phone use is a real issue at times – maybe something really important is happening on social media but can it really not wait an hour or two? We have a social life too (apparently!) and yet we still turn our phone onto silent in classes. And, just as we have a job to do, so do you!!

- Don't waste people's time/remember other people's time is important – if you can't make a meeting, then say so but otherwise make sure you come prepared and are on time. If you are going to be late or miss a meeting, try to give notice. Again, think about how you would feel if this happened to you. Say, for example, you are gathering data for your final-year project and your participants just don't show up. How annoying, how unprofessional! How you hope they find a dead bug in their sandwich for this hideous offence against you! Grab hold of that feeling and use it to make sure you are on time!!

- Remember to ask if you want your tutor to be a referee – not only is this polite but you may find we can't actually complete a reference form without explicit permission from you owing to data protection laws. Also, if we don't feel able to provide you with a reference, we have the right to say 'no'!

Activity 4.1: Practice makes perfect!

We have talked a lot about professionalism and many of the tips we have given you are easy to deliver (e.g. turn up to class!). However, what do you do if something awkward crops up? Something difficult? To help you practise your skills we have developed the following scenarios. Have a read and think about how you might respond to these issues in a professional way. Example answers are provided at the end of the chapter.

Scenario 1: You are unhappy with a grade and want to know why you got the feedback you did. You decide to contact the marker. How do you approach them and what do you say?

Scenario 2: You want to do some work experience. How do you go about setting this up?

Scenario 3: You need an extension for a piece of coursework. Draft an email to the administration team (or whoever manages extensions at your University) to apply for this.

Scenario 4: You overhear students talking about a member of staff in a derogatory way. What do you do?

Of course, there will be plenty of opportunities to demonstrate your professionalism and to practise these skills. Always have an eye on this and make sure you consider how to approach issues appropriately and professionally when they come up. This can be challenging to do – especially if you are stressed – but remember you don't want to be that student your lecturer remembers for all the wrong reasons! You want to be the one they remember as polite, engaged, enthusiastic, and (above all) professional.

Chapter resources

For **up-to-date standards and guides**, see the BPS website: https://www.bps.org.uk/our-members/standards-and-guidelines

For more on **prospects**, see: https://www.prospects.ac.uk/careers-advice/interview-tips/how-to-prepare-for-an-interview

For more information on **continuing professional development**, see: https://www.bps.org.uk/our-members/professional-development

For more on **BPS membership**, see: https://www.bps.org.uk/join-us/membership

Activity 4.1: Example answers

Scenario 1: Things *not* to do (at least one of us has experienced each of the following!):

- Write an abusive email complaining about your grade
- Storm into the marker's office without knocking and start shouting
- Make rude comments about the marker to other students/staff, in person, via email, or via the online learning platform (e.g. Moodle, Aula, Canvas, Blackboard)

Here is how you might go about it: (1) Take some time out, you are upset and it is hard to focus on how to react if feelings are running high. (2) Re-read your feedback to see if you missed something the first time around that might explain your grade. (3) If you do decide to contact the marker, email them to ask for clarification and/or a meeting to help you understand why you got the grade you did. (4) If such a meeting is arranged, prepare in advance questions that you would like to ask your marker. (5) LISTEN to what they say. (6) Ask for specific advice about how you could do better next time. For instance, if they say you need more critical evaluation, then ask for an example of where you could have expanded your critique; if the feedback is to evidence base your work more robustly, ask for examples of where additional citations should have been included.

Scenario 2: There will be different support services available at different Universities, but we would be very surprised if there is not a careers service somewhere and this is a good place to start. Often, the careers service is located near the library but might be in the Student Union. Once you have found the service, contact them to ask about opportunities. Even better, set up a meeting. Prepare for this meeting by listing the kinds of jobs/roles you are interested in. If you are not sure, this is fine but do think about what skills you want to develop. This can help you look for something you are interested in. For example, if you want to work with young people, perhaps look for opportunities at a school, sports club, or youth support organisation. When you have identified an opportunity you are interested in, make sure you make contact in their preferred way (email, using electronic application form). Follow the instructions carefully – for example, if you are instructed not to include a CV, then don't include one! It might be tempting but, as an employer, the first thing that tells them is that you can't follow basic instructions. Not a good first impression! Make sure you know how long you are likely to need to wait for a response and make a note to follow up after a reasonable amount of time has passed. For example, if they say it takes up to two weeks to process applications, do not follow up after a week. If you are asked for interview, your careers service should be able to support you to prepare (e.g. arrange a mock interview).

   Another approach to searching for work experience might be to approach your tutors to see if they are aware of any opportunities. We know of organisations that students have had good experiences with and can send lists/website links to these. Amy has done this numerous times for Forensic Psychology students, as it can be a little daunting to know where to start and/or you might not know what is available locally if you are new to the area. Don't be disheartened if staff signpost you to Careers – this just means they don't have anything to hand that fits what you are looking for. A good tutor will always signpost where they can. Your tutors are busy people, so you might not get a reply straightaway; however, they won't mind answering careers emails (in fact, these are some of our favourites!). Also, don't be afraid to follow up if you don't hear anything after, say, a week. It is likely we forgot to reply (in Amy's case at least!) rather than had no intention of doing so.

Scenario 3: The easiest way to apply for an extension is via email. There will usually be a form to complete. Here is an example of an email template:

> Dear [insert name],
>
> I have been unwell over the past week and have been unable to complete my [module name] coursework due on [insert date]. Please find attached my application for an extension for this piece of coursework plus a letter from my GP showing that I have been ill.
>
> I hope to hear from you soon.
>
> Kind regards
> [name]
> [student number and course]
>
> [Attachments: completed application form for an extension and a GP letter as evidence you were unwell]

If you are not able to find a form, you can still send an email – for example, something like this:

> Dear [insert name],
>
> I have been unwell over the past week and have been unable to complete my [module name] coursework due on [insert date]. I am not sure how to apply for an extension for this coursework. Are you able to advise what I need to do? Thank you.
>
> I hope to hear from you soon.
>
> Kind regards
> [name]
> [student number and course]
>
> [Attachment: GP letter as evidence you were unwell]

***Scenario 4*:** It is not your responsibility to call out this kind of behaviour directly, but it would be sensible to report this to your course director (your institution may use different terms), as the behaviour of all students reflects on us. We don't want to be the University or the course with the reputation for bad student (or staff!) behaviour – this can have a negative effect on the opportunities of future students. For example, if someone is rude to a guest speaker, they are unlikely to return the following year; or if someone doesn't take their work experience seriously, the organisation might withdraw their offer to future year groups. Overhearing someone being rude is also awkward and uncomfortable for you and may disrupt or damage your own learning experience. Therefore, you will find that staff will take your concerns seriously. There will be a policy on how to report problematic behaviour at your institution. This might entail sending an email directly to your course director (see below for an example). If you are unsure how to report such behaviour, or prefer not to do so directly, you could contact your student representative (there is usually at least one per year group on a Psychology course) and ask them to act on your behalf; or you could ask a trusted tutor to make the course director aware.

Dear [insert course director name],

I am a student on [course name] and have some concerns about the behaviour of some of my peers. Would I be able to arrange a meeting with you to discuss please?

Best wishes
[student name]
[student number and course]

5 Learning from experience and digesting feedback

You may have heard of 'reflection' or 'learning from feedback' previously. In this chapter we will cover what it means to be a 'reflective learner', and how you can learn through experience and feedback throughout your degree. Ultimately, we hope to support you in using reflective learning to develop yourself, learn to manage change, and deal effectively with setbacks. It will help you boost your grades too!

Overview of topics

- What is reflection?
- What do we mean by being a reflective learner?
- Why should I be learning from experience and reflecting? How will this help me in the future?
- How do I reflect?
- How can I learn from experience during my time at University?
- Dealing with change
- Dealing with setbacks

Learning outcomes

1 To understand what it means to be a reflective learner
2 To understand how reflection can support you in the future
3 To develop knowledge about how you can learn from experience, manage change, and deal with setbacks

What is reflection?

Essentially, reflective practice means taking our experiences as a starting point for learning. By thinking about them in a purposeful way – using the reflective processes – we come to understand our experiences differently and take action as a result.

– Jasper (2013, p. 1)

What do we mean by being a reflective learner?

As a concept, reflection can seem a little bit scary! It is a key skill in Psychology and so embracing reflection is a good idea. Basically, resistance is futile! Hopefully, once we have discussed what it is, how it can be done, and why it's important, it won't seem so daunting. Here, we provide a short introduction to the concept. You will probably do a number of reflections as part of your degree (giving you a chance to practise your skills) plus there are lots of additional resources you can use to develop and refine your reflective skills (see the list of resources at the end of this chapter).

Common reactions we get when we occasionally set reflection as an assignment include: 'I hate reflections', 'what's the point?', and 'I'm terrible at reflection'. We get it, we really do, reflection doesn't always come easily to some and might not be the most exciting assignment you'll ever be set. But if these thoughts cross your mind, hold your horses, calm down, and think about why we ask you to reflect – you need to learn how to develop your skills, and reflection is the best way to do this!

So, let's get started. Imagine you are in a seminar at University and your tutor asks you to do a presentation on a topic of your choice. You complete the presentation and sit back down, and never think about the presentation again. If you don't think about what you did well, what you didn't do so well, and what you could do in the future, then how will you do better next time? The answer is, you won't. You will continue to make the same mistakes over and over again, and wonder why you receive the same (possibly bad) grade. In addition, if you don't take the opportunity to improve your skills now, it could impact on your job options – for example, if a presentation is needed as part of an interview. But if you were to deliver your presentation, sit back down, and then think about what just happened – what went well, what didn't go so well, what other options were open to you, what support you could have sought, what actions you need to take to improve – you would be reflecting! And this will help you the next time you have to deliver a presentation.

Why should I be learning from experience and reflecting? How will this help me in the future?

There will be plenty of opportunities for you to learn from experience whilst at University, not just when you are asked to do an assignment on the topic! These include engaging in both practical and theoretical learning, where you will get feedback for your performance and ideas. We will cover different types of feedback in the next section, but for now let's look at why you should be learning from experience.

As we noted earlier, if you don't reflect, you are likely to continue to make the same mistakes and risk performing poorly as you progress to more challenging assignments (e.g. getting low grades, or even getting yourself into a sticky situation such as sharing your work with the same friend who got you into trouble for academic misconduct on a previous occasion; see Chapter 8 on academic integrity for more information). However, rather than focus on the negatives, let's think about what could go *right* if you reflect.

The University environment allows you to make some mistakes (not monumental ones – we obviously don't condone illegal behaviour or rule-breaking) so that you can learn and grow. This means that by making mistakes, getting feedback and reflecting on this, you can identify your own strengths and those areas that require further development, better preparing you for the future. The workplace might be challenging at times, and you can use the reflective skills you learn at University to manage tricky situations.

So, by teaching about reflection we're actually trying to prepare you for your future. We are trying to help you develop yourself, and develop your knowledge and skills. We want to encourage you to try to change your way of thinking about learning through experience and reflection – see it as investing in your future, and showing self-care through *becoming the best version of yourself.*

Speaking of becoming the best version of yourself, now is a good time to talk about comparing your reflections, and the grades you receive, with those of others. It's human nature to look to others and compare, but there are times when this is really unhelpful, especially when it comes to your learning. We commonly hear from students: 'Me and my friend reflected on the same thing and got different grades, why is that?' First, we would expect reflections to be individual pieces of work, and personal, so it would be unlikely two people would experience the same thing in the same way and then write it up the same. Second, we wouldn't expect you to get the same grades as you should be writing up work independently! There could be a number of reasons why two students got different grades. For example, you focused on different things, in varying degrees of detail, or one of you may not have fully completed the steps needed to reflect in depth. Either way, it is important not to compare yourself to others, but rather compare yourself to yourself – so that you improve and learn from your experience.

How do I reflect?

Much like anything in life, there are many ways you can go about reflecting. You might want to reflect (see what we did there?!☐) on the model that works best for you.

Gibbs' cycle

One of the most widely used models of reflection is Gibbs' cycle, originally developed in 1988. This cycle of reflection works on a cyclical 'loop', where you work through each step to help you better understand a particular situation, and

Figure 5.1 Gibbs' cycle

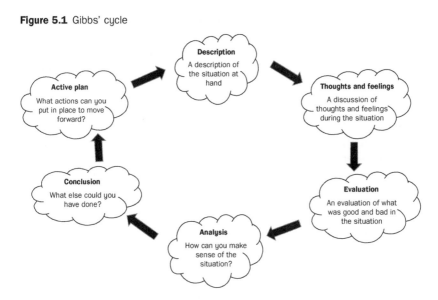

put together an action plan to support skill development in the future. Figure 5.1 provides a visual representation of the model.

As you can see, you must complete each step before moving onto the next one. If you don't provide enough (or too much) detail, the reflection won't make much sense, and won't be very good in helping you understand the situation and develop from it. In our experience, students tend to spend a lot of time on the 'situation', providing unnecessary mundane information, such as 'before I went to University I went to the shop and got a coffee'. Take some time to think: 'does this really help me understand the situation at hand?' Also, it is really important to have a clear action plan; simply stating 'I will work on this' is not enough – *how* will you work on it? Be specific.

Here is an example reflection using the sub-headings from Gibbs' cycle:

Situation: We were asked to complete a presentation for our assessment at University. We were required to follow the assignment brief by choosing one mental health issue, and then discuss and evaluate appropriate treatment for an individual with that mental health issue. I failed and got the feedback that I spoke too quickly, I did not go into enough detail about the mental health issue, and did not critically evaluate.

Thoughts and feelings: Initially I was upset when seeing my grade; it was not as I had expected, and I thought I had done okay. Following this, I began to feel embarrassed, but also angry at myself for not fully following the assignment brief, and letting my nerves get the better of me. Once I had taken some time to calm down, I felt more relaxed, and I was able to sit down and reflect on this experience, so I could put an action plan in place for my resit presentation.

Evaluation: In any situation there are both positive and not so positive aspects. In this instance, the not so positive aspects were failing the assignment, and the feelings of upset and anger I experienced after seeing my grade. However, the positive of this situation is the opportunity to get feedback for my presentation, which I can now use to work on my future presentations, and which will also help me when it comes to resitting the assignment.

Analysis: As a shy individual, I'm always nervous at the idea of giving presentations. Looking back at the situation, I ignored the presentation assignment until a week before it was due, leaving me very little time to prepare, and to practise delivering it. According to Eysenck et al. (2007, p. 336), anxiety can have a negative impact on how we perform in cognitive tasks. As such, because I had previously failed a presentation, my levels of anxiety for the current presentation were elevated. This resulted in my avoidance of the assignment and the feelings of anxiety it caused me, which resulted in poor preparation and delivery.

Conclusion: Upon reflection, I had other options that I could have chosen instead of procrastinating. I could have spoken to my tutor about my anxiety and asked for support for this; they may have been able to provide me with some hints or tips. I could have planned the presentation better, ensuring I followed the assignment brief fully, and practised delivering it with a friend or family member until I felt confident. I also could have re-familiarised myself with the lecture and seminar material to ensure that I knew what I was doing for the assignment, and read through the assignment marking guide.

Action plan: Next time I will make sure I read all the guidance before starting my assignment; this will ensure that I know what I am doing, and if I am unsure I will ask my tutor specific questions about the assignment. I will then create a timeline for the assignment, and ensure I stick to it so that I have plenty of time to complete the presentation – and practise it. According to Bandura's (1977, p. 194) self-efficacy theory, we avoid situations that we think are threatening. However, if I am to complete my degree I am unable to avoid tasks such as presentations. Therefore, in order to reduce the 'threat' of presentations, I will ensure that I practise delivering them, and seek feedback from friends or family members. In particular, I will ask for feedback on the content of my presentation and the pace at which I deliver it. In the short term, however, I will practise the same presentation again and deliver this in front of my family or friends next week with the aim to improve my pacing and delivery.

Hopefully this example reflection shows you one way of reflecting. You will notice that there is a strong emphasis on the action plan at the end, where it is important to be specific as to what you will do next, and give a timeframe! Your reflections will be individual to you, and you can reflect on anything!

How can I learn from experience during my time at University?

One way of learning from experience during your studies is to listen to the feedback you are getting. First, throughout the course of your degree, you will get a lot of verbal feedback from staff, such as during lectures (if live) and seminars, from your personal tutors and supervisors. One example of verbal feedback occurs when you are doing activities in seminars. For instance, you might respond to a question or feed back your work to the class, and the tutor will give you feedback on your progress, quite often in a 'things-you-did-well' and 'things-you-can-work-on' sort of way. While this may not be graded, verbal feedback is really important, as it allows you to check your own progress and understanding. Remember, just because it's not written down doesn't mean it isn't important, so make sure you listen to what your tutors have to say! Also, it's useful to make notes, so you can reflect on the feedback later.

'Formative' tasks are opportunities to complete an activity (usually related in some way to your assignment) and gain feedback from staff, and sometimes from other students. This is a really valuable way of allowing you to 'give it a go', without the pressure of a grade, and get feedback before you go ahead and complete your summative work. Examples include practice tests and peer review activities on assignments. These are really useful for spotting when you are going down a rabbit hole, i.e. not focusing on answering the question set. By listening to formative feedback, not only will you avoid failing your assignment by missing the brief but you could also potentially boost your grade.

Summative assignments are the assignments that are graded and should come with written feedback (in the text and/or as a feedback page). Usually, you will get feedback on the aspects of the work you did well, and what you need to work on to achieve a higher grade. These are the assignments that will count towards your degree classification.

So, how do you process the feedback, and what should you do if you don't understand? These are good questions! Sometimes a grade, or feedback, can come as a shock, especially if you haven't achieved the grade you thought you would. First and foremost, before you go 'all guns blazing' to senior members of staff to complain, please read your feedback (and this includes any in-text comments), leave it for a couple of days (once you have had the time to cool off), and read it again. Having done this, it can be really useful to book an appointment with your marker to discuss the feedback; sometimes written feedback can appear harsher than when delivered in person. Discussing feedback is especially important if there is something you don't understand – seeking clarification of what the issue was and/or examples of something (e.g. what you could have critiqued in more depth) is useful to help you understand areas that need developing. It is also absolutely essential if you need to resit an assignment – you don't want to fail your second attempt because you didn't understand what went wrong the first time. Once you have this feedback, spend some time reflecting on what you might need to do in your future assignments, and then write down an action plan (and revisit this when you start your next assessment).

Marking and moderation

Sometimes students find it hard to understand the marking process. This can be especially difficult if you receive a grade you are not pleased with. However, rest assured that all Universities follow a formal process when marking students' work. Typically, this will involve:

1 Tutors mark your work according to the assignment brief and marking criteria (which should be made clear to you throughout your module).
2 A sample of all markers' work is moderated. This does not mean second marking, but rather a means to ensure that markers are marking correctly against the marking criteria, and to ensure they are being consistent and fair.
3 An external examiner will also look at a sample of marked work, to ensure consistency and fairness in marking. They will also ensure that the materials available to students and markers is suitable, as is the material delivered by tutors.

Dealing with change

We all experience change from time to time. Sometimes these changes can be difficult to deal with, and they might be unwelcome. But this is part of life, and you may experience some change whilst you are studying. A great example is the Covid-19 pandemic that began in 2020, when the world came to a standstill and everything we were used to changed completely. Students across the world suddenly had to learn everything online, and staff were asked to learn new technologies at a moment's notice to facilitate online learning. So, if we can't predict or stop change, what can we do about it? In many instances, nothing. We can't change the fact there is a global pandemic but we can work proactively to problem-solve and find solutions. In the case of the pandemic, this involved embracing the idea of online learning and working to understand the new way of working.

We also need to think about how we can cope with change. It is difficult but there are ways we can prepare ourselves for the unexpected. There's a concept called 'resilience', which is the ability to 'bounce back' from difficult events, and turn negative experiences into a learning opportunity. Having resilience is incredibly important in Psychology in particular. For example, you may decide to work with victims of crime, but if you lack resilience, you will spend most of your time re-living painful events (e.g. dwelling on traumatic stories told by victims) and being incredibly unhappy. There are lots of resources that can support us in developing resilience (see the resources at the end of the chapter).

Another part of dealing with change is taking responsibility – for yourself and your wellbeing. What we mean by this is being able to identify when you are struggling with something, and doing something about it! For example, if you are finding a particular type of assessment difficult, it is important to identify what you can do to work on it, who you can ask for support, and how to put your action plan in place. This is about you taking responsibility for your own learning (and wellbeing), whilst working on your resilience too. Also, it is common for people to blame external factors for failures – and students are no different when looking for a reason why they failed an assignment! For example, struggling with the change from first to second year. This might be relevant, but you are missing a trick if you don't also reflect on what you could have done differently, and if you were struggling, what you could have done to support yourself and manage change. None of us is perfect, so it really is important to reflect!

Dealing with setbacks

Setbacks are common – at University, at work, and in life in general! There are, however, many ways to deal with setbacks. It would be impossible for us to provide an answer to every possible scenario, but what we can do is give some examples of times when things have not gone so well and what we did about it.

The first example is something a lot of people may be able to relate to, not getting your dream job. It is very, very unusual (and lucky) to apply for your dream job straight out of University and actually get it. Often it can take years and a lot of experience to achieve your goal. Let us each give you an example!

First, Rachael was very excited when applying for a lecturer post at a University, but unfortunately did not even get an interview. At first, she was upset but soon decided to seek feedback from the individual reviewing the applications, and asked that they communicate any future opportunities. Rachael came to realise that she needed some management experience, and further guest lecturer experience. So, rather than wallowing in self-pity and giving up on her goal, she took heed of the feedback and re-applied six months later. This time she was successful in securing an interview, and felt better equipped having the skills required for the role. In hindsight, having an extra six months' experience has helped her be successful in the role.

Dan's example concerns his experience of studying for a PhD. The original idea for the PhD was to explore certain psychological interventions that may be beneficial in helping individuals with a diagnosis of psychosis to cope with feelings of ostracism (i.e. being ignored and/or excluded). He spent a year developing a strong rationale for his research as both theory and literature suggested that this particular population would be the most at risk of being ignored (due to lay perceptions of dangerousness) and the most affected by such feelings. After waiting over a year to obtain NHS ethics clearance to recruit from hospital wards, Dan got the opportunity to interview participants – to confirm that people with a diagnosis of psychosis do in fact experience these events. It was important to qualify this if Dan was to proceed with potential intervention studies. However, almost half-way through the PhD, one by one the participants stated: 'I do not feel ignored'. This left Dan in a predicament to say the least: 'Aargh! I am halfway through my PhD and my thesis has a major flaw'. This was a really crucial moment. Despite the anxiety this caused him, it was pivotal for Dan to change the focus of his PhD away from certain groups being affected to people's *perception* of being ostracised. This change in direction led Dan to a new line of research and the realisation that perception is critically important, which helped him defend his thesis during the viva. So, viewing setbacks as an opportunity can help you to push forward and be successful.

Finally, Amy has had a few setbacks, including being made redundant and being the reserve candidate (basically she came second!) after a number of good interviews. However, it is the outcome of one event from early in her career that set her on a path that, on reflection, she is much better suited to. Having seen an advert for a role at a prison, Amy contacted the recruitment team for an application form. However, the person she spoke to refused to send her one, stating that as the deadline was only a few days away Amy wouldn't have enough time to complete and return it. Amy insisted she could and asked for the form again but was refused. Without any means to get to the recruitment office to pick up a hard copy of the forms, Amy was unable to apply. She felt that her chance of a good job opportunity was basically blocked by someone who couldn't be bothered to email her an application form.

A few days later, however, Amy came across a really exciting opportunity in a research role. She applied and – by some miracle! – got the job, a post in which she fell in love with research. Even better, the job was based in a police station and so she was able to learn about policing from the professionals (she refers to this as 'learning by osmosis', as there is nothing better than being embedded in an environment you want to learn about). On reflection, she simply would not be where she is today without that job. In hindsight, and having now conducted research interviews with people in prison, she is not convinced working in a prison would have been for her. So, that rude (and unprofessional) member of the recruitment team inadvertently did Amy a favour!

Setting myself goals

An important aspect of reflection, and dealing with feedback, is thinking about what you could do differently in the future to improve. One way of doing this is through setting yourself goals. For example: if you know you struggle with critical evaluation, you might want to set yourself a goal around attending a critical evaluation workshop, or getting feedback from a member of staff. Goal-setting is important to ensure that you learn from your experiences, and make changes to become a better version of yourself.

SMART goal

You might hear someone talking about creating a SMART. This is a great way of identifying your short-, medium-, and long-term goals, and mapping out how you will achieve those goals. For more information and handy tips, visit:

https://www.mindtools.com/pages/article/smart-goals.htm

To start using SMART goals, see Chapter 10.

Take home message

Reflection is an important part of your learning journey. It helps you think about your own strengths and limitations, and what you need to work on. Off the back of reflection, setting yourself SMART goals will also benefit you personally and academically by allowing you to think about what you need to do next to become the best version of yourself.

Activity 5.1: Gibbs' quiz

Without looking at previous content, link the steps in Figure 5.2 to the correct label and explanation.

Figure 5.2 Gibbs' quiz

Step 1	Feelings	What was good or bad about the situation?
Step 2	Action plan	How did you make sense of the situation?
Step 3	Analysis	What will you do next time?
Step 4	Description	What did you think and feel?
Step 5	Evaluation	What happened?
Step 6	Conclusion	What else could have been done?

Chapter resources

On **reflective writing**, see the University of Edinburgh 'reflection toolkit': www.ed.ac.uk/reflection/reflectors-toolkit/all-tools

Mind have some really useful resources around managing stress and **building resilience**: www.mind.org.uk/information-support/types-of-mental-health-problems/stress/developing-resilience/

For **SMART goals**, see: https://www.mindtools.com/pages/article/smart-goals.htm

References

Bandura, A. (1977). Self-efficacy: Toward a unifying theory of behavioral change. *Psychological Review, 84*(2), 191–215. https://doi.org/10.1037/0033-295X.84.2.191

Eysenck, M.W., Derakshan, N., Santos, R., & Calvo, M.G. (2007). Anxiety and cognitive performance: Attentional control theory. *Emotion, 7*(2), 336–353. https://doi.org/10.1037/1528-3542.7.2.336

Jasper, M. (2013). *Beginning reflective practice* (2nd edition). Cengage Learning.

Activity 5.1: Answers

Compare your answers with Figure 5.3.

Figure 5.3 Gibbs' quiz: solution

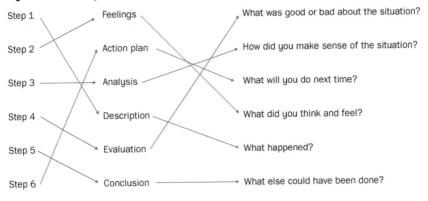

6 Research methods: why are they important?

Understanding research methods is an essential part of your development as a Psychologist. This chapter is not intended to teach you research methods (e.g. research design, quantitative or qualitative analyses). Instead, it will explain what research methods are, why they are important, and how they will help you understand other elements of Psychology. Our aim is to help you manage any anxiety you have about research methods – also known as 'the stats fear'.

Overview of topics

- What are research methods?
- Why is engaging with research methods important?
- What can I do to prepare?

> **Learning outcomes**
> 1 To understand why a good grasp of research methods is an essential part of becoming a Psychologist
> 2 To identify strategies to help prepare for learning research methods
> 3 To ease anxiety (e.g. the 'stats fear') to reduce any impact on performance

What are research methods?

'Research methods' is a rather broad term. Indeed, research methods covers elements of research design, methods of data collection, analysis (quantitative, qualitative, mixed methods), as well as other criteria such as the philosophical approach to research, sampling strategies, and ethics. It would be impossible to cover everything in a single chapter, as it takes a whole book just to cover statistical analysis – as you will see from your University library! What we will do here is make the distinction between quantitative and qualitative research to help introduce you to the key approaches to research. To keep it interesting, we'll use some applied examples – you know, real-world stuff!

So, what do we mean by quantitative research? Well, often as researchers, we need to collect data that is quantifiable (i.e. able to be expressed as a quantity). Here, the data (e.g. a measure of an attitude or opinion) are reduced to a single numerical score so that we can test our hypotheses or predictions about psychological phenomena. For example, it is common in quantitative research to collect information in the form of scores on a questionnaire (e.g. a personality inventory, a measure of psychological distress), health information such as heart rate, blood pressure, etc., even the frequency score of how many times your favourite TV show is advertised. In contrast, qualitative research focuses on collecting data using people's own words (e.g. transcripts from interviews, focus groups) to understand how they experience psychological events, although this is not to case for all qualitative research. It can be confusing for students to decide between a quantitative or a qualitative design. However, it should be pretty straightforward, since your *research question* will dictate which approach you take!

To illustrate the importance of the research question to your choice of research design, let us consider some examples. If you wanted to know *if* a weight management programme has been successful (i.e. if people had lost weight), you could use a quantitative design. For example, you could measure the participants' weight and/or body mass index (BMI) at baseline and at the end of the programme to determine if there has been any significant reduction in weight or BMI. However, if you wanted to know *why* the programme was or was not successful, you would need to use a qualitative design – for example, ask the participants if they followed the programme, and which parts of the programme were considered useful.

Now let's take another example. If we wanted to know whether perceived ostracism (i.e. feeling ignored or excluded) is a psychologically distressing experience, we could interview people who have been ostracised or often feel disconnected from others. Here, we would adopt a qualitative design. If, however, we were interested in determining whether ostracism is *associated* with psychological distress, we would adopt a quantitative design. Specifically, we could measure perceived ostracism and psychological distress using questionnaires and see if the scores are related (i.e. whether participants who score high on ostracism also score high on psychological distress). But what if we wanted to explore whether ostracism *causes* psychological pain or distress? We could randomise people to an exclusion condition (e.g. they are rejected) or an inclusion condition (i.e. they are accepted) to see if there is a meaningful difference (referred to as a *statistically significant* difference) in the average scores between the two conditions on a measure of psychological pain. In both of these scenarios (correlational design, experimental design) we would be collecting quantitative data, but remember it is the research question which decides the approach to be taken.

Research in Psychology is exciting and allows us to explore a range of different phenomena. To do research in Psychology, it is essential that you have an understanding of research methods. In our experience, however, many students view research methods (typically in relation to quantitative approaches) as either dull or too difficult compared with other subjects taught on their Psychology course. Consequently, some students may disengage from the topic, procrastinate, or even desist from learning, particularly in relation to quantitative analyses and statistics. This is often due to statistics anxiety, colloquially known as 'stats fear' (Macher et al., 2015), whereby a student feels inadequate regarding statistics, mathematics, or the use of statistics software such as SPSS. The problem is that disengaging or procrastinating only makes stats fear worse. You focus so much on not being able to do stats that you miss the opportunities to learn. It is then hard to catch up and the more behind you get, the more you worry. It's a vicious cycle. It is, therefore, especially important to attend research methods classes because the more you learn, the more you will understand the topic and the more your fears will be allayed. The other problem with stats fear is that it can lead to some students preferring the so-called 'easier' option by putting more time, energy, and attention into learning qualitative over quantitative research methods and analyses. However, it is important for students to have a good understanding of both approaches, as the way you design your study or analyse your results will be ultimately determined by your research question – so a good knowledge of one approach won't suffice. Moreover, the idea that qualitative research is easier is a myth! Both approaches have their strengths and limitations. For instance, when analysing qualitative data you will not need to use any statistics, but it can be very time-consuming collecting, transcribing, and coding the data, and there are also several checks to ensure the rigour of your analysis just as with quantitative analyses. When students discuss research proposals for their dissertation there is often a tendency to pick whichever method/approach is considered the easiest. We would recommend you focus instead on the topic which you find interesting and that your choice of method be guided by your research question – not the other way around.

Why is engaging with research methods important?

The completion of research methods modules is a standard requirement of all BPS accredited courses. However, we don't want you to do research methods just because you have to. Okay, we know that there is no escape and so we could say you might as well bite the bullet and throw yourself into learning about it. But that is short-sighted. We want you to fall in love with research methods (alright, maybe not in love but at least have a grudging acceptance for how great it is!). Research is fundamental to advances in Psychology and so you do need to know how it works and be able to critique it. So, let's talk about why it is so important to engage with research methods.

To begin with, understanding elements such as research design will allow you to determine whether a piece of research adopted the correct approach – and subsequently the correct form of analysis. For example, if a researcher wanted to know *why* an intervention worked, but adopted a quantitative design, it is clear they adopted the wrong approach. Furthermore, learning research methods will provide you with a platform to be able to critically evaluate research studies. For instance, you will be able to evaluate the design of a study, understand the results, and cast a critical eye over any conclusions that have been drawn by the researchers. Moreover, knowing about the strengths and limitations of a research design will give you the opportunity to be creative – for example, you might suggest how to improve the design of the study. Would a qualitative approach be better? Perhaps different questionnaire measures could be used? Would an additional control help to make the results more valid? Such skills will help you in your academic assignments as well as your longer-term career in Psychology. Indeed, knowing how to critically analyse a research paper will aid you in developing a convincing and well-developed rationale (for a study) or argument (for an essay). There will be more discussion on how to develop a convincing rationale in Chapter 9.

As Psychologists, we cannot take research at face value but need to be able to identify what the strengths and limitations of any study are to determine whether the research can be trusted. This is very important, as there have been concerns over the reliability of the findings of Psychology research studies in the past. For example, in a sample of 30,717 Psychology articles published in top journals between 1985 and 2013, one in eight papers contained a major error in its statistical reporting (Nuijten et al., 2016). So, this would mean that for every eight Psychology papers you read from that period, there is a possibility that one of them will report a significant (or meaningful) effect, when in reality there wasn't one! Furthermore, Psychology is also facing a replication crisis in that up to two-thirds of major psychological research findings have *not been replicated* (Open Science Collaboration, 2015). The problem here is that, without replication, we can't determine whether the original findings are robust. As such, there is added scrutiny now to ensure that only high-quality Psychology research is conducted (and published), partly in an attempt to rebuild and ensure the integrity of the discipline. Therefore, equipping yourself with an understanding of research methods is essential not only for your development, but to prepare yourself to defend your work rigorously throughout your career.

Another reason why it is important to connect with research methods is to evidence your understanding of them when you come to complete your dissertation project. All Psychologists are expected to design and conduct an independent piece of empirical research. If you have a sound understanding of research methods, and you can conduct and report your analyses well, your project will be all the better for it. Plus, given that your dissertation is often heavily weighted in Psychology courses, doing well in it could be the difference between a 2:1 and a first! We would also encourage you to think about the potential to publish your dissertation once you have finished your degree. Aim as high as you can from the outset. The first step in this process is to speak to your supervisor to see whether your idea is novel and/or whether your rationale is convincing enough (e.g. a sound replication design). You also need to ensure that the method is strong, since you cannot correct methodological flaws once the data have been collected – 'Whoops! I really should have included an additional questionnaire measure here'. Therefore, it is important that you critically consider your design *before* you collect your data. When you have your data, you will need to show that you have followed all the necessary methodological steps to ensure they are reliable and that your report is accurate. To facilitate this, you can consult the relevant research methods text.

The next section will detail some guidance on how you can prepare for your learning of research methods.

What can I do to prepare?

We have observed certain traits in students who succeed in research methods modules (we will focus specifically on quantitative analyses here) and in those who experience difficulties (see Table 6.1). As discussed earlier, many students experience the 'stats fear' and consequently disengage with their learning of research methods. This can lead to avoidance behaviours such as missing lectures and workshops, not persisting with activities involving datasets when things become challenging, procrastinating (e.g. switching to an episode of *Game of Thrones* instead), and so on. Unfortunately, although such techniques may bring short-term relief, they will only make your journey of learning statistics more difficult in the long term. Indeed, it's like stepping into quicksand: the more you struggle, the more stuck you become. The key is to try to remain still and avoid the initial fear until you are rescued. In the context of statistics, you need to persist with the activity or ask for support rather than letting the stats fear endure!

When preparing to learn research methods we would recommend you try a range of different materials. Let us start with book resources. There are several published books in your library (or virtual library) to guide you through the basics of what you need to know before moving onto more complex topics. Some authors write in a style and use examples that would suit some students rather than others. As such, it would be good practice to read an example chapter from at least a couple of sources to see which you prefer. This is also useful if you find yourself needing further clarity for a particular analysis. Sometimes it can be helpful to read two or three different chapters about the same topic to see different examples to help your understanding. Your tutor will suggest an essential text for you to read. This will be the minimum you have to read to complement the lecture content. However, you are also recommended to source a secondary text which suits you.

Some students, however, may find it difficult learning by reading books alone. Indeed, some students prefer learning through listening to podcasts, watching videos, or having practical experience (e.g. with statistics software). Universities have moved towards online (or blended) learning. As such, you may have access to your tutor's lectures which you can watch (or listen to) whenever you wish. You may consider supplementing these audio-visual materials with additional sources which you find independently (e.g. Professor

Table 6.1   Behaviours of students who succeed or struggle when learning research methods

Succeed	Struggle
Attending/engaging with lectures and workshops	Not engaging with the lectures or workshops (or attempting to catch up)
Using lecture materials or textbook as a guide when experiencing difficulties with SPSS	Procrastinating when having difficulties with SPSS (e.g. not downloading the materials, loading up SPSS, or starting activities) and waiting for the instructor to provide a visual demonstration to the class
Asking questions to clarify understanding	Not asking questions and/or not engaging with material that can support learning during a workshop
Engaging with additional activities (e.g. quizzes, datasets, padlets, virtual learning platform posts)	Only completing the bare minimum (i.e. completing assignments) without any additional revision or engagement in learning activities
Doing additional reading (e.g. sourcing articles published in academic journals in the last 3–5 years) on top of the main background reading	Either not reading the assignment brief correctly or only sticking to a single background source
Using peer-reviewed articles as templates when writing research reports (including the results sections)	Writing a research report without the correct structure (i.e. not following the APA conventions)
Taking the extra step of providing all the main statistics in the results section as well as providing additional calculations (e.g. effect sizes)	Presenting a research report bereft of such detail

Andy Field has a series of excellent recorded lectures and videos on statistics made available on his YouTube channel). The workshops are used to consolidate your learning. To help prepare for workshops, you could ask for the dataset which your lecturer used to illustrate how to run a particular analysis, and then run the analysis yourself. You may also find it useful to change the labels/variables to something more relatable. For example, when introducing analyses, we sometimes include popular culture references such as *Game of Thrones* to illustrate a novel experiment.

Let us take a step back and remember the stats fear. Students may not engage successfully with learning statistics due to the fear of being incompetent with maths. It is important to note, however, that *there actually is not much maths involved*. When writing a results section (for a quantitative analysis) you will notice there are certain values (e.g. the p-value) that need to be reported. However, let's break down an example scenario to see what is really needed in such a report. Imagine that we (as researchers) want to examine whether watching a TV series could cause an increase in how awesome a person rates themselves. Let us assume here we actually have a reliable and valid measure of 'awesomeness'. Participants are randomised to watch one of three TV series (let's say a boxset of a season): *Game of Thrones* (GOT), *The Crown*, and *East-Enders*. What do we actually need to know in the results section? We need to know whether there are any differences in the average scores (i.e. the descriptive statistics) by looking at the mean (i.e. the average). For example, it could be that those in the GOT condition score higher in awesomeness than in the other two conditions. What this does not tell us is whether there is a meaningful difference. As such, we would then do a statistical test (in this case a one-way ANOVA as we have three conditions/groups/levels). This allows us to provide a p-value (a probability value) to conclude whether there actually has been an effect (a significant effect). What you need to know primarily is whether your p-value is above or below a certain threshold. If the p-value is less than .05 (e.g. $p = .049$), then there is a *statistically significant difference*. If it is greater than .05 (e.g. $p = .051$), then there is no significant difference. This will allow you to either support or reject a hypothesis that you propose. Of course, there are other steps to include here in your report (e.g. checking your parametric assumptions, post hoc analyses where appropriate), but as you see there is little maths involved. You need to know where to obtain the values you need and be able to interpret them correctly (and your lecture notes/textbooks will show you how to do this). In fact, the only real maths you would use would be calculating an effect size (e.g. Cohen's d), which tells us how big or small the effect is. Although we may detect that there has been a significant effect, it is important to understand the strength of the effect. Indeed, imagine that the mean score (of a depression questionnaire) for a group of patients is 29.9 after an intervention but before the intervention the mean score was 31. A fairly trivial effect! Helpfully, there are spreadsheets and online calculators that can calculate the effect size for you. We would therefore recommend you follow step-by-step instructions from your chosen learning resources to know where to find the key values you need. You should also try to practise your analyses with different datasets. Take up the option to practise with any optional activities within your lectures and workshops to consolidate your learning.

Although it is good to know there isn't as much maths involved as previously imagined, there still can be anxiety when confronted with research methods in the moment (e.g. I am sitting in front of a computer having palpitations about what I am expected to do ... help!!). What is the best way to deal with this? First, take a deep breath – panicking will only cloud your thinking. Try to calm yourself and focus on what you want to find out. We suggest trying to find the answer independently to start with (e.g. search different sources) but if you cannot find the answer, then ask your tutor for support. If you do not understand the answer, then ask the tutor to perhaps rephrase in a different way or provide a different example – remember, finding out the answer is only part of what you want to know, understanding *why* it is the right answer is also essential. This will help you deepen your understanding.

You will also have other support services available to you (e.g. most Universities provide additional statistics support workshops as drop-ins for students). However, do not forget that all analyses are conducted in a step-by-step fashion. It is okay to pause after a step, take a break, to look something up and then come back to it again when you have found the answer. You will notice as you go through your research methods module that the same steps will apply for most analyses within the same class (e.g. if checking for significant mean differences, you typically follow the same steps in principle). As such, you will notice that as the weeks go by, the analyses will start to make more and more sense.

One other key tip we would encourage you to follow is to use peer-reviewed articles as a template when writing your report. For example, if you have a key Psychology paper that is the main source for your assignment, pay attention to how the authors have shaped their argument as well as how they structured all other necessary sections (abstract, methods, results, discussion, etc.). There is more guidance on peer-reviewed articles in Chapter 8.

Activity 6.1: Write below the top three things you learned from this chapter.

Chapter resources

Discovering statistics resource: https://www.discoveringstatistics.com/statistics-hell-p/

References

Macher, D., Papousek, I., Ruggeri, K., & Paechter, M. (2015). Statistics anxiety and performance: Blessings in disguise. *Frontiers in Psychology, 6*, 1116. https://doi.org/10.3389/fpsyg.2015.01116

Nuijten, M.B., Hartgerink, C.H., Van Assen, M.A., Epskamp, S., & Wicherts, J.M. (2016). The prevalence of statistical reporting errors in Psychology (1985–2013). *Behavior Research Methods, 48*(4), 1205–1226. https://doi.org/10.3758/s13428-015-0664-2

Open Science Collaboration (2015). Estimating the reproducibility of psychological science. *Science, 349*(6251). https://doi.org/10.1126/science.aac4716

Activity 6.1: Example answer

There is no example answer for Activity 6.1, as what one learns varies from person to person, depending on existing knowledge. We hope, at least, you are feeling confident that stats anxiety is normal but completely 'overcomeable' – is that even a word? Mmm, maybe not, but then surely every Psychologist has to make up a word once in their career ... not sure this is Amy's best attempt but we'll run with it!

7 | Effective research strategies and utilising the library

This chapter will look at what 'literature' is, why it is important, and what literature researching skills you should develop during the course of your degree. We will discuss how you can develop those skills from the outset, including: how to make the most of the library, why reading, reading, and (yes you guessed it!) even more reading is important, how to search for articles/books/journals, and how to make effective notes. We also impress upon you the importance of basing your arguments on evidence, signposting you to other relevant chapters in the book.

Overview of topics

- What is empirical literature?
- Why is literature important?
- How to search for literature effectively
- How to make effective notes

Learning outcomes

1 To understand how to use the library to help search for relevant empirical literature
2 To understand why literature is important when constructing an evidence-based argument
3 To understand how to take effective notes

What is empirical literature?

You will often hear your tutors talk about the need to refer to *relevant* empirical psychological literature in your assignments. What does this mean? Well, let's break it down. Literature includes the sources you choose to use in your assignments to support your arguments. If you make a claim – say, *'Game of Thrones* is the best TV show ever' – you need to support this with some evidence (e.g. statistics, awards) and facts, and citing a source makes your argument even stronger. But for an academic piece of work you need to cite *reliable* sources in order to get the best grades. What do we mean by reliable? Well, if you were to cite evidence from a peer-reviewed journal (e.g. an article reporting a rigorously conducted experiment) to support your argument, this would be more trustworthy than citing a newspaper report or opinion piece – more on this later.

So, what do we mean by psychological literature? Sometimes students lose marks in their essays or dissertations because they fail to use references that have direct relevance to Psychology. Although it is of course okay to cite sources outside Psychology to provide a general introduction to a topic, you must ensure you incorporate theory and research evidence that is clearly Psychology-based – it is a Psychology degree you are studying for after all! In summary, therefore, relevant empirical psychological literature means reliable sources that provide evidence to support the main argument you are making, and to *answer the question that has been asked*; it is not about what you found interesting or proving how much you have read! You are bound to read work that is unrelated to what you are investigating, or not relevant to your specific research question. It is important that you do not include all the sources that you read to showcase your knowledge of the topic area – focus only on those that directly answer the question at hand and are most *relevant* for your argument. Your tutors know that a quality essay involves reading more literature than you actually cite in your reference list.

It is easy to claim something in your essay about some psychological phenomenon or behaviour – for example, when a person believes they are being ignored, this makes them angry or sad. It makes sense, right? It seems logical. However, it would be much better to provide evidence in support of such a statement (a reference to a relevant theory, say, and to strengthen your claim further, a peer-reviewed research study which demonstrates that being ignored could lead to such emotional reactions). Imagine, for example, that you are a Forensic Psychologist working in the field and you are challenged in court ('where is your proof of this?') when asked to present your evidence. You can't just say, 'well, it's logical isn't it' – your credibility as a professional would be questioned and your reputation potentially tarnished! Citing reliable sources to support your claims not only shows that you have a good understanding of the topic in question, but also provides you with the platform to defend your views and claims.

So, what would be considered reliable evidence? When trying to support or contradict a theory, you should cite research from a peer-reviewed journal – research that has been reviewed and accepted by experts in the field. In our experience, students tend to come to University having used books as their primary source for all their written assignments. However, as you progress through your Psychology course you will start to become familiar with peer-reviewed journals and use them as your main literature source. You will find a wide range of research methods in the articles you read, including experiments, surveys, interviews, observation – and many more! – all of which would be worthy of consideration. Included within the category of reliable resources are review articles (e.g. systematic literature reviews). Such reviews are an account of the state of the literature relating to a particular topic (e.g. What are the current theories and evidence relating to social rejection right now? What are the debates on the topic?). Review articles are excellent in helping you to understand the literature at a glance (you do not need to read every paper on the topic!), and for 'setting the scene' for your assignment.

Peer-reviewed articles are generally the best sources for you to base your evidence on, but there are others you can use, including:

- Textbooks: these might provide a core theoretical source, or an overview of a relevant research method or analysis procedure.
- Secondary sources: research cited by the author of the article/textbook you are reading; however, you should always read the original work.
- Government reports: be aware of who funded the work when reading the conclusions, as there is the potential for these to be biased!
- Charity research: for example, research from the perspective of service users.
- Office for National Statistics (ONS): a provider of national statistics that might help you to highlight a real-world problem. As you will know, ONS figures are often quoted in the news – but be careful, news outlets may not have interpreted the information correctly or put 'spin' on the numbers. Always look up the original source!
- Government legislation/policy: helpful sources when quoting a key definition.

Peer-reviewed journals

So that only high-quality, original research appears in academic journals, all papers submitted for publication must go through a rigorous peer-review process – assuming they meet the journal's criteria for publication in the first place. When a paper is sent for peer-review, at least two experts will review and comment on it to decide whether it merits publication.

Although a good source of information, it is important to remember that there may be a delay between submission of a research paper by its authors, and its publication in a peer-reviewed journal. In fact, it is quite common for the process to take a year or more. This might mean there is a gap in the knowledge, since there may have been changes in the law, attitudes, and/or technology since the paper was written. For example, with developments in technology, new opportunities to commit crime emerge, and researchers will need time to identify these new crimes and conduct empirical research on them. In such cases, you might need to draw on more than the academic literature to build your argument. However, if you choose to use non-academic sources, make sure you are extra careful to critique this literature in your assignment. For example, let's say you are writing an essay about cybercrime, and you choose to cite the website of a financial institution or cybercrime prevention organisation. It may contain relevant content, but it could be opinion-based – and what would that mean for the strength of your argument? It could be that the opinions are those of professionals/experts, which would hold some weight, but it would have been better if they could have backed up their opinions with evidence (e.g. prevalence statistics, internal reports).

Okay, so now you know what sources you should use, let's look at what you should be wary of.

After several years of marking students' essays and dissertations, we have noticed a common theme in those that are not up to scratch. These students either do not include any evidence to support their claims, or they include the *wrong* sources. Look at the list of sources below commonly included in such assignments but which are considered poor quality evidence:

- Wikipedia
- *Psychology Today*
- Newspaper articles – unless the work you are doing is on media portrayals of Psychology-relevant material, e.g. stigma, prejudice
- Blogs

Activity 7.1: Why do you think we advise you to avoid the above sources?

Why is literature important?

Is it really that important to include literature and citations in your essay? You might think, 'if I know the relevant theory and I know how to answer the essay question, will I still get a good grade even if I don't add any references?'. Some students believe that references are simply 'marked' as part of writing style criteria – wrong! In order to score well on critical argument, you need to ensure you *cite sources to support your argument*. Moreover, to get the top grades, you also need to provide the *best possible* evidence. We will provide you with strategies on how to do this later in the chapter, but first let us consider how certain claims can actually be quite damaging.

Imagine that a student attends a lecture on rape myths (i.e. holding a prejudicial or false belief against the victims of rape). They are asked to address the question 'Do rape myths exist?' and they make the claim that disabled persons who are sexually assaulted see it as some kind of 'favour'. This is an incredibly insensitive statement and has the potential to cause distress to the reader. If such a claim were to make it into print or be broadcast, it could be very harmful since it not only endorses rape myths but could lead to a rise in sexual assaults against disabled individuals. Moreover, such a claim is unsupported and does not take account of relevant literature on victim-blaming culture (e.g. Taylor, 2020).

Now that we can see how an insensitive and unsupported claim can be damaging, what about citing a newspaper article as a key source of evidence? Surely, you might think, such evidence must be okay, as newspaper articles provide an account based on key sources. Well, consider the following true example. In 2016, *The New York Times* published an article in which it was suggested that when older adults have regular sex, this can help prevent dementia (O'Neill, 2016). Older adults reading this article might be encouraged to increase their sexual activity, and suggest having sex with their partners – after all, it would help prevent the couple developing dementia! On the surface, the article appears reliable since O'Neill was referencing a peer-reviewed paper published in the journal *Age and Ageing* (Wright & Jenks, 2016), and included direct quotes by the authors. However, Wright and Jenks (2016) did not actually recruit participants with dementia, *or make any claims about preventing dementia* ... they highlighted that regular sex in a healthy ageing population is linked with improved cognitive function. So, the newspaper was misrepresenting the findings of a published study. This is just one of many cases in which newspapers have misrepresented the findings of psychological research. That is why it is so important that you read and reference the original source rather than a newspaper article (or other online blogs and resources) in your assignments.

So, we have seen that unsupported, insensitive, and inaccurate claims have the potential to be harmful. Let us now consider a good example of how to support your argument. A student is writing an essay and is making the following claim: 'Being ignored and excluded (i.e. ostracised) is known to be a painful experience and causes people to have lower self-esteem'. Notice that there are two key elements to this statement: ostracism is (1) painful and (2) results in a loss of self-esteem. As such, at least two sources should be cited to back-up these claims. What sources might be relevant? Perhaps a qualitative study reporting how people express how ostracism is painful (e.g. Waldeck et al., 2015), and an experimental study showing how, when people are rejected in a ball-toss game, they report a significant reduction in self-esteem (e.g. Zadro et al., 2004). Citing such sources would strengthen the claims, but is there anything that could make the argument even stronger? If bringing attention to the effects of ostracism is to be a focal part of the essay, then the student might consider providing a theoretical account of *why* ostracism has adverse effects. In other words, the student could choose a relevant theory, explain how it can be applied to the effects of ostracism, and cite it in their essay. Now armed with some support for the claims being made, how can the student attain top marks? They need to show evidence that they have read widely. One of the references they cite is from 2004, and so is relatively outdated. Is there any more recent evidence to support their claims? Or *contradict* them? Citing up-to-date references really shows you are in touch and informed. What's more, when you read the most up-to-date empirical sources (e.g. systematic reviews, research studies), you can get ideas for further research as well as grasp the limitations of your study and/or the study area. So, by using such sources you can also strengthen your critical evaluation, which will help you boost your grades!

How to search for literature effectively

When you begin University, you will be introduced to a range of academic services that can support you during your degree. One of the essential services (if not the most essential!) is the library. A University library holds a range of relevant resources (e.g. textbooks, access to journal articles, former dissertation projects) that will help you gain a greater understanding of Psychology. Moreover, each year your lecturers speak with the subject librarians to order the most relevant resources for you to access. Most libraries also have an inter-library loan service so you can access sources even if they are not held by your own University library.

It is important to remember that a library is not just a stack of books. There are lots of other resources and opportunities for you to learn new skills (e.g. academic writing, referencing). You may find it difficult at times to search for literature effectively, or study in general. It can be helpful to have a quiet and peaceful place to study, away from your housemate and his Xbox or your children's play area! One way of doing this is to book some space in the library. Also, don't forget library staff do more than simply welcome you into the building and scan your books in and out, they can help you track down those eusive sources you really need and can't find. They are experienced in retrieving data and can guide you not only to search for a specific source but show you how you can do more complicated searches in the future. What if you aren't sure exactly what you are looking for? Librarians use their reference interview skills and experience to help figure out exactly what you need. All University libraries have their own database where you can locate and retrieve resources (electronic or hard-copy), and they can lend a helping hand so you can get to know how to use the system correctly.

Let's now consider an example of how to search for literature effectively. You have just been given an essay with the title, 'Critically evaluate whether Psychotherapy is effective'. You will have your lecture notes, perhaps seminar materials, and a relevant textbook/chapter that you have been signposted to by your tutor. These are all useful for developing your understanding of the topic. What you need to do next is to search for relevant articles to support your arguments (e.g. evidence to show that Psychotherapy *is* or *is not* effective). One common strategy is to look at the key source (e.g. journal article) highlighted by your tutor, and then read the papers in that source's reference list. This is very handy as you can include in your assignment relevant references that helped to shape this key article. However, this strategy would not demonstrate your capacity to search the wider or the most recent empirical literature. To do this, you can select from a range of sources (e.g. searching key terms on PsychINFO, Google Scholar, PubMed). Using Google Scholar as an example, you first need to identify relevant key words (e.g. Psychotherapy, efficacy, interventions, effectiveness) to help you narrow down your search – let's go with 'Psychotherapy effectiveness'. If you were type this search term into Google Scholar, it would give you roughly 1.3 million sources. Suffice to say it would take a rather long time (more than that needed to watch the complete box set of *Game of Thrones*) to read through all these articles and select the right evidence for your argument. Helpfully, Google Scholar lists the top entries on the first page. Although some of these could be outdated, they will be the most widely cited. You can also narrow down your search based on the year articles were published – quite useful if you only want the most up-to-date research in the field!

It is possible to restrict your search terms further by using Boolean operators (i.e. using 'AND', 'OR', and 'NOT'). If you want to search for evidence of whether a particular form of Psychotherapy is effective, you could be selective in using operators. For instance, if you searched for 'cognitive behavioural therapy (CBT) effectiveness NOT mindfulness interventions', you would only see articles related to CBT and not to mindfulness interventions. For further guidance on restricting your search terms and using Boolean operators, see 'Finding what you need: Tips for using PsycINFO effectively' (https://www.apa.org/science/about/psa/2013/10/using-psycinfo).

Now, let's say you have pinpointed quite a few articles that you have found to be relevant (and some not so much!). It can be quite tricky keeping track of those articles, so it is important to keep notes on them. It is also useful to record the DOI number, if the article has one, as this will help you to track it down again later. Get into the habit of keeping copies of papers in a logical online filing system (e.g. Rayyan), and recording the details of the key papers in software such as EndNote. It will save you a lot of time if you extract only the key information (or citation data) from relevant journal websites, and it will be there for you to manage at the end of your assignment. Dan wished he had done this for his PhD, as although he had cited key sources in the text (in-text citations) he hadn't created his reference list. When he came to do this a few months later, it took him two days to track down most of the sources – but as he couldn't locate all the original sources, more reading and literature searching was required. In short, using such software can be a real time saver and helps you be more organised – and should prevent you from losing anything.

How to make effective notes

When searching for literature, it is important that you make effective notes as you go. The last thing you want is to have spent a day reading through and sorting relevant articles, to then not be able to read your own handwriting (we are all guilty of this!) or not understand the key points you were trying to record about those articles, meaning you will have to read them all again! But why make notes at all? Well, it can help you understand a particular concept, theory, model, or key research study in more detail. The key to making good notes is to ensure you write down the *most important* information (e.g. key words, concepts, key research findings, the author's conclusion from the study) and ignore the rest. It can also be quite helpful to make your notes more visually appealing (e.g. colour-code key words, concepts). You can also record a summary of what you have read – in written form or audio-recorded – to help you remember the key points of the text. Moreover, to be more critical, note down your thoughts about the work, such as whether you agree with the conclusions of the study.

You also need to be clear about the question you are trying to answer. Being focused on answering the question (i.e. is Psychotherapy effective?) will not only help you identify what you need to read, but also to read critically. You should also aim to make your notes specific to answering your research question. It could be that you keep coming back to the same papers, so colour-coding or dating your notes might also be helpful. There are a range of different resources available to help you improve your note-taking, and you will have academic writing support available to you that provides tips and guidance on how to take notes.

We will leave you with a final pointer here – when making notes, we recommend that you paraphrase appropriately. In other words, do not copy word for word chunks of the original text (or if you do, use quotes in your notes so you know this is what was said by the original author and not your interpretation of it). In your final assignment, you need to summarise the key findings in your own words! If you do not paraphrase others' work appropriately, your assignment may be flagged by relevant similarity-checking software and you run the risk of disciplinary action for suspected plagiarism. Fortunately, we provide guidance in Chapter 8 on how to paraphrase correctly and ensure your academic integrity!

Take home message

It is really important for your development and performance to ensure you include relevant psychological literature to support your arguments. Failing to include such evidence will not only show your work lacks a critical argument, but could also result in you getting a low grade or worse (there is more on critical writing in Chapter 9). Also, in addition to the key resources made available to you by your tutor, try to locate the most recent (contemporary) evidence to back up the claims you are trying to make!

Activity 7.2: Apply what you have learned

To finish this chapter, apply what you have learned. Think of a hot topic in Psychology that you want to search the literature about, or perhaps you have been given an essay title and you need to start compiling your evidence. Use the relevant search engines to find good-quality contemporary studies that support a particular position (e.g. Psychotherapy is effective) and others that don't (e.g. a particular Psychotherapy or Psychotherapy in general is ineffective). As a final tip, you may consider using a document such as the Critical Appraisal Skills Programme (CASP) checklist to help you evaluate the quality of the sources you have found.

Chapter resources

For **library research** in Psychology, see: https://www.apa.org/education/undergrad/library-research

For tips on using **PsychINFO and Boolean operators**, see: https://www.apa.org/science/about/psa/2013/10/using-psycinfo

References

O'Neill, N. (2016). Hot sex makes you smarter, study finds. *New York Post*, 15 February. https://nypost.com/2016/02/15/hot-sex-could-make-you-smarter-study-finds/

Taylor, J. (2020). *Why women are blamed for everything: Exposing the culture of victim-blaming*. Constable.

Waldeck, D., Tyndall, I., & Chmiel, N. (2015). Resilience to ostracism: A qualitative inquiry. *The Qualitative Report*, *20*(10), 1646–1670. https://doi.org/10.46743/2160-3715/2015.2346

Wright, H., & Jenks, R.A. (2016). Sex on the brain! Associations between sexual activity and cognitive function in older age, *Age and Ageing*, *45*(2), 313–317. https://doi.org/10.1093/ageing/afv197

Zadro, L., Williams, K.D., & Richardson, R. (2004). How low can you go? Ostracism by a computer is sufficient to lower self-reported levels of belonging, control, self-esteem, and meaningful existence. *Journal of Experimental Social Psychology*, *40*(4), 560–567. https://doi.org/10.1016/j.jesp.2003.11.006

Activity 7.1: Example answer

The main reason that you should avoid sources such as websites and newspaper articles is that they are not peer-reviewed. As such, you really cannot tell how good or how bad the evidence is, or assess the quality of the source material/information. You will often find that websites are opinion-based, and news articles can be skewed and misrepresent the evidence. You should always read and refer to the original source (e.g. for a key research study) rather than take as gospel what is said on a website or in a newspaper article. This will help show that you can form your own conclusions about a piece of research. Using original empirical findings to develop your academic arguments can help you demonstrate integrity, while appropriate paraphrasing will help you avoid any potential misconduct (e.g. plagiarism). There is more on how to ensure your academic integrity in Chapter 8.

We also find that some students, particularly in their first year of study, have a tendency to include lecture materials or seminar materials as a primary reference in their essays (i.e. they cite these as sources). Although, there is nothing wrong with this approach (at least at first!), do remember that it is best for you to source the original articles and talk about these in your own words.

Activity 7.2: Example answer

Hopefully you will have found a range of different resources relevant to your topic. The key to picking the right resources it to screen them based on whether they help you to answer your research question. Using a tool such as the CASP checklist will also help you to evaluate the quality of the research (e.g. Was there a clear research question? Was the methodology sound? Are the results clear?). Remember, you want to include good quality and relevant literature to support your arguments!

8 Academic integrity and referencing

In this chapter we will focus on what academic integrity is, and provide some real-life examples of scenarios and ethical dilemmas you may face whilst at University. Additionally, we will explore what referencing is, why it is important, potential outcomes if there is academic misconduct, and signpost you to resources that may be helpful as every University has its own referencing procedures. We will address plagiarism and integrity but also 'finding your own academic voice' and demonstrating a depth of understanding of the topic you are writing about.

Overview of topics

- What is academic integrity?
- Plagiarism and collusion
- What is Turnitin?
- Academic conduct process
- Referencing
- Ethical integrity
- Carrying academic integrity forward into your professional career

---

Learning outcomes

1 To understand what academic integrity is and why it is important
2 To develop skills to successfully avoid plagiarism and collusion
3 To understand how academic integrity feeds into your future career plans

---

What is academic integrity?

Academic integrity means acting with the values of honesty, trust, fairness, respect and responsibility in learning, teaching and research.
    – University of South Australia, Exemplary Academic Integrity Project

Academic integrity applies to everyone – tutors, researchers, and students – so it is important you understand this, as it will be something to be aware of throughout your career. Key aspects are to act honestly, take responsibility for your actions, and show fairness in every part of your work.

Academic integrity is important for reputation (University of South Australia, n.d.) and so it will not surprise you to learn that it is taken very seriously by Universities, Higher Education bodies (e.g. the Higher Education Academy and the Quality Assurance Agency for Higher Education), and professional organisations (e.g. the British Psychological Society). The key area for concern is plagiarism but there are also other issues to consider, including collusion, data fabrication, and cheating in exams.

Plagiarism and collusion

Some issues are pretty simple to understand, such as cheating in exams (i.e. any attempt to gain credits/grades/marks in a dishonest way). However, other concepts you might not be so familiar with. This chapter will cover two key concerns for Universities – plagiarism and collusion – not only to help you understand what they are but, crucially, how to avoid them.

Plagiarism

So, what is plagiarism? Plagiarism is when someone takes something from someone else and inserts it in their work, and either claims it as their own or fails to make the source clear (see Figure 8.1). This can be intentional (i.e. the author deliberately uses the words or ideas of someone else) or unintentional (i.e. there is no deliberate attempt to mislead but a failure to acknowledge the source). However, be aware that unintentional plagiarism is still a concern – it does not matter whether you did or did not mean to plagiarise, if you present work as yours when it isn't, then this is a problem. You need to ensure you don't misrepresent yourself and that you are clear what your ideas are based on (i.e. you must cite supporting references).

Figure 8.1 What is plagiarism?

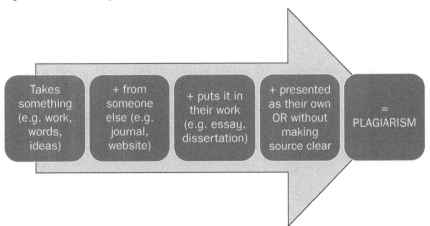

You should also be aware of self-plagiarism – that is, you cannot resubmit work you have previously received credit for (Williams & Davis, 2017). Put simply, you can't hand in the same piece of work for multiple assignments hoping to receive credit for the same work multiple times. Some students think they can take a short cut by choosing similar topics for their assignments, but remember – no two assignments will ever be exactly the same, even if they are on the same topic. Taking a short cut will likely entail you missing the point and doing poorly anyway.

Activity 8.1: Is this plagiarism?

Look at the examples below. Would any of these be considered plagiarism? If so, why? (Check your answers at the end of the chapter)

Example 1

What the original says	What the student writes	Is this plagiarism?
Successful crime linkage can increase the quantity and quality of evidence available to the police (Ashmore-Hills et al., 2017), which increases the likelihood of apprehending and successfully prosecuting repeat offenders (Grubin et al., 2001).	Successful crime linkage can increase the quantity and quality of evidence available to the police (Ashmore-Hills et al., 2017), which increases the likelihood of apprehending and successfully prosecuting repeat offenders (Grubin et al., 2001).	

Example 2

What the original says	What the student writes	Is this plagiarism?
Successful crime linkage can increase the quantity and quality of evidence available to the police (Ashmore-Hills et al., 2017), which increases the likelihood of apprehending and successfully prosecuting repeat offenders (Grubin et al., 2001).	Crime linkage can boost the quality and quantity of evidence available to law enforcement (Ashmore-Hills et al., 2017), which upsurges the prospect of catching and successfully prosecuting repeat criminals (Grubin et al., 2001).	

Example 3

What the original says	What the student writes	Is this plagiarism?
Successful crime linkage can increase the quantity and quality of evidence available to the police (Ashmore-Hills et al., 2017), which increases the likelihood of apprehending and successfully prosecuting repeat offenders (Grubin et al., 2001).	Crime linkage can be used to support law enforcement to capture and prosecute repeat offenders. This is achieved through an improvement in the amount of good quality evidence identified in serial cases (Burrell & Tonkin, 2020).	

Note: The original source in all three examples above is Burrell and Tonkin (2020).

Collusion

Okay, so what is collusion? Collusion is when students collaborate with each other to complete an assignment and hand in the same (or very similar) piece of work. This includes helping someone else to plagiarise – that is, allowing another student access to your work. Where matching between students is identified, both are likely to be referred for investigation for collusion. We are not saying don't do group work and you can and should ask others for help and advice if you need it. However, this help should be to *support* you to do the work rather than have the work done for you (Williams & Davis, 2017).

Activity 8.2: When working together, what is acceptable?

Take a look at the table below. Which of these activities is acceptable group work? Make notes and then check your answers at the end of the chapter.

Activity	Acceptable or not?
Working in the library together	
Lending someone an assignment	
Testing each other (e.g. exam revision)	
Asking someone to help you write an assignment	
Borrowing an assignment	

Activity	Acceptable or not?
Discussing lectures with peers	
Uploading your assignment to an essay-sharing website	
Sharing references/papers with peers	
Discussing feedback	
Using someone else's assignment as the basis for your own	
Group work where you have explicitly been told to produce a single, joint report	
Writing joint notes with a peer that would be the basis for an assignment (e.g. content and structure)	
Sharing memory sticks with peers	

Key point

Ignorance is *not* an excuse. You should therefore take the time to understand what plagiarism and collusion are so you can take steps to avoid both.

What is Turnitin?

Universities take issues of academic integrity very seriously and use technology to help them detect possible cases of plagiarism. The most widely used is called Turnitin. This is a plug-in that is attached to assignment submission portals in your University's virtual learning platform (i.e. the submission points on Moodle, Aula, Canvas, or Blackboard). What happens is, when you submit an assignment, it is compared to an existing database of assignments from those Universities where Turnitin is used, which is 98% of Universities in the UK (https://www.turnitin.com/regions/uk/university) – so you can imagine how large this archive of past papers is! Turnitin also checks online sources (e.g. websites, blog pages, etc.). If it finds a match to an existing source, it will highlight this. It will do this for all matches and then produce a report so readers can see where matches come from. This report provides a final percentage score indicating the proportion of the work that matches other sources. This report is used by academic staff to determine if there is an issue with plagiarism or collusion. This is important because some matches won't be an issue (see Table 8.1 for some examples of legitimate and illegitimate matches).

Table 8.1 Legitimate and illegitimate matches

Legitimate matches: not a sign of plagiarism	Illegitimate matches: a possible sign of plagiarism that might need to be investigated
• Correctly cited quotes • Correctly formatted references in the reference list • Matches to an assignment template provided by your tutor	• Quoting directly from text without making this clear (i.e. *not* using quotation marks and not including the citation)

Whilst Turnitin can help to detect plagiarism, it is *not* a plagiarism checker. Instead, it is used to support decision-making around suspected cases of plagiarism. It is a means of assessing the similarity between texts and of assessing if academic misconduct (i.e. plagiarism, collusion) might have occurred. However, although Turnitin can highlight matches, it is members of staff who use their academic judgement to determine whether matches are acceptable within the context of the particular assignment. If the matches are legitimate (e.g. involve reference lists, a template, correct use of quotes), then this is fine. If they are not legitimate (e.g. uncited quotes, text lifted from other sources), this will be considered for investigation for academic misconduct. From your point of view, you need to be confident that any matches in your submission are for legitimate reasons and not the result of poor academic practice (e.g. poor citation) or cheating (e.g. copying another student).

A common question we are asked is, 'what Turnitin score is allowed?' We won't beat around the bush here – trying to determine an appropriate similarity score is like asking, 'how long is a piece of string?'. There is no correct answer – if someone tells you otherwise, they are either misinformed or lying to you! The bottom line is that there are so many factors that can impact on similarity (length of assignment, whether there is a template, including a published scale in the appendices, reference lists, etc.), that there is no magic number! We have seen Turnitin scores of 70% that were not an issue (e.g. a short assignment with a long reference list) and others with scores of 10% that were – in one case two students handed in different essays but with the same word-for-word conclusion, including the same spelling mistakes! This was investigated and found to be a case of collusion. What is important is that, if there are any matches, these are legitimate: if this is the case, then you will be fine; if not, you could find yourself being investigated for suspected academic misconduct. The consequences of this can be severe, so please do make sure you understand how to write, reference, and evidence-base your work correctly.

Many Universities will offer you the chance to hand in a draft of your assignment so you can access a Turnitin report for that work. Please use this opportunity if it is offered to you and make time to look at matches and understand why they are there and if they are a problem. Sometimes students don't do this because they worry that their final piece of work will match their draft on the database. But don't worry about this. Tutors can switch on a draft function, allowing your draft to be compared to the Turnitin repository but not uploaded to it. Once your final summative assignment is uploaded to the repository, it will be used as a point of comparison for all other submissions going forward. Cool, huh?!! So, the bottom line is, take the opportunity to check your work. If you have difficultly interpreting your Turnitin report, you must ask a tutor to help you. It is essential you understand what is and what is not permitted to match. Ignorance is not an excuse when it comes to plagiarism so, even if you plagiarise accidentally, you might still find yourself in trouble.

Academic conduct process

It is worth saying something here about the academic conduct process. The specifics will vary from institution to institution but the general process will proceed something like this:

1 Tutor identifies potential issue with student work (e.g. suspected plagiarism or collusion). This may be the result of possible illegitimate matches on a Turnitin report but could also be flagged in other ways (e.g. marker identifies two similar-looking essays).
2 Student is referred to academic conduct office for investigation.
3 An independent Academic Conduct Officer (ACO) – or equivalent – is assigned to the case. This will be someone trained in academic integrity issues but not part of your department so as to ensure independence of process.
4 The ACO investigates the case – this might be done on paper but usually they will invite the student involved to a meeting to discuss the issue.
5 A decision is made: there is or is not a case to answer. Outcomes will vary depending on whether there is a case to answer (i.e. plagiarism or collusion has occurred) and the severity of the misconduct. Examples of possible outcomes for cases of misconduct include: 0% score for the assignment, 0% score for the whole module, written warning letters, referral to an academic learning assignment (e.g. a good practice quiz on avoiding academic conduct), temporary exclusion, or (in the most severe cases and/or where there is an escalation of outcomes) permanent exclusion.
6 Often the ACO will also provide verbal warnings and advice about how to avoid issues going forward.
7 If there is no case to answer, the investigation will be concluded. With no plagiarism/collusion having occurred (or insufficient evidence of this), you can simply move on with your degree. However, it is still worth listening to any advice given (e.g. opportunities to improve academic practice).

If you find yourself being referred for suspected academic misconduct, then please bear the following in mind:

- Don't panic – it is natural to worry about what this might mean for you but try to stay calm. Ask for information.
- Speak to the Student Union/Student Advice Centre (or equivalent) – they can offer support to help you through the process (e.g. advice on procedure, help to prepare for meetings).
- Engage with the process – don't ignore it hoping it will go away. Attend any meetings you are asked to attend, find out what the issues are, and tell your side of the story.
- Trust the process – if you haven't done anything wrong, the investigation will conclude there is no case to answer.
- Remember that ignorance is no excuse – if you have done something by accident, it will still be deemed an issue. In such cases, it is best to be honest and learn from your mistake.
- Use the process as an opportunity to learn – ACOs and tutors want you to do well. We don't like referring and investigating cases. Aside from the paperwork it can be distressing for all involved. You should find the process supportive as staff work with you to help you develop your skills and avoid plagiarism/collusion in the future.

Let's now look at the best ways to avoid plagiarism and collusion.

Top tips!

- Get into good habits (see Figure 8.2).

Figure 8.2 Getting into good habits

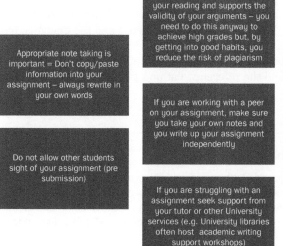
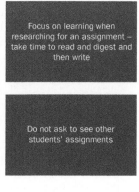

Appropriate note taking is important = Don't copy/paste information into your assignment – always rewrite in your own words

Remember citation evidences your reading and supports the validity of your arguments – you need to do this anyway to achieve high grades but, by getting into good habits, you reduce the risk of plagiarism

Focus on learning when researching for an assignment – take time to read and digest and then write

Do not allow other students sight of your assignment (pre submission)

If you are working with a peer on your assignment, make sure you take your own notes and you write up your assignment independently

Do not ask to see other students' assignments

If you are struggling with an assignment seek support from your tutor or other University services (e.g. University libraries often host academic writing support workshops)

- Make sure you understand what you are writing about – some people plagiarise or collude because they are not confident in their understanding of the content.
- Ensure you reference appropriately in the text.
- This sounds obvious but don't pay someone else to write your essay – just because essay-writing services are available does not mean that they are allowed!!

To quote or not to quote?

The most common thing students do to try to avoid plagiarism is to quote everything. Whilst this does mean you are less likely to plagiarise, it can lead to a tendency to overuse. The problem with this is that it only shows you can find information but not that you understand it. Overuse leads to essays being disjointed and (sometimes) not answering the question, which will obviously have an effect on your grade. It is important you learn to (a) paraphrase properly and (b) write things in your own words. Do not use a quote as a substitute for the point you are making. Demonstrate understanding of the quote by making sure you explain the argument it is helping you to make.

Referencing

We talked about the importance of basing your arguments on evidence in Chapter 7. We primarily discuss this in relation to ensure ensuring your work is of good quality so you can achieve your best grades. However, good practice in referencing will also help you avoid plagiarism.

Referencing provides the reader with the source(s) of your information. As such, the reference is the link between what you write and the evidence base for your argument. It is essential that you reference your arguments throughout your work – this will be in the form of in-text references (you will find some examples in this book!) and the reference list you provide at the end of your assignment.

Reference list vs. Bibliography

Reference lists provide a list of all sources (e.g. journal papers, books) which you directly cite in your assignment. **Bibliographies** provide both the sources you have directly cited and the background reading for the assignment. Note that, as a Psychologist, you are likely to be asked for a reference list rather than a bibliography.

Just to make things more confusing, there are different styles of referencing (e.g. APA, Oxford, Harvard, Chicago, etc.). But whatever style is used, the references will provide the same key information: who the authors are, the date of publication, the name of the paper/chapter, and in what journal/book it was published. The different styles just do it in slightly different ways, which basically means formatting the references differently; often this simply means using commas or brackets in different places! The two most important things to remember are: (1) make sure you include references in the text and in a reference list at the end of your work, and (2) that you use the correct format for the style required. As Psychologists you are likely to be asked to use APA (American Psychological Society) referencing style (see https://apastyle.apa.org/). There are lots of guideline documents available to help you do this. There are a couple of things you need to be aware of though. First, guidelines are updated, so make sure you are using the most up-to-date version (ask your library or tutor what this is). Second, if you read non-Psychology journals, you may find their reference lists are formatted differently – so make sure you re-format any references in your assignment using the correct (APA) style.

It is also worth noting that APA have good practice guidelines for things like bias-free language, how numbers are presented (e.g. number of decimal places used), and how to format tables. They have comprehensive guidelines on how to structure research reports too. You may be asked to follow these guidelines, so it is worth being aware of them. See https://apastyle.apa.org/ under Style and Grammar Guidelines for more information.

Ethical integrity

It is important to note that academic integrity extends to ethical integrity. We have already discussed expected standards of behaviour in Chapter 3, but it is important to be conscious of ethics when considering academic integrity too. This is not just ensuring you adhere to standards and codes of practice (e.g. BPS Code of Ethics and Conduct) but also that you do not misrepresent your work. Data falsification (i.e. manipulating data to give a false impression of outcomes) and data fabrication (i.e. making up data or research findings) are not unknown and Universities take these very seriously. Some students might be tempted to 'make up' a few participants or try to gear their data analysis to reach a particular outcome when they are thinking about deadlines and grades. However, this is unacceptable behaviour and would also be referred for investigation for academic misconduct. It is imperative that you present work accurately. In research, it does not matter what you find or if you find evidence for your hypothesis; what matters is that you present a legitimate outcome. This is the only way research really moves our understanding forward. And, before you ask, yes you can get a good grade with a small sample. We're not saying aim for that but so much of your grade is about how you design, deliver, interpret, and write up your findings. A small sample alone will not prevent you from doing well.

Carrying academic integrity forward into your professional career

It is important to carry what you learn at University, including academic integrity, forward into your professional career. Remember, your degree course is just the start of being professional (see Chapters 3 and 4), and the onus is on you to continue this. This doesn't just apply to your written work but should cascade down into all areas of your professional life. For example, you need to be aware of potential power imbalances when gathering data for research purposes – if people feel obliged to take part, this is not voluntary and you are not behaving with integrity.

Take home message

Remember ignorance is **not** an excuse for academic misconduct. It is **your** responsibility to understand what constitutes academic dishonesty. If you are not sure you **must** ask.

Activity 8.3: Write three things in the box below you could do to avoid plagiarism and collusion after reading this chapter.

Chapter resources

For information on the **APA referencing style**, see: https://apastyle.apa.org/

For the **Exemplary Academic Integrity Project/Academic Integrity Policy Toolkit** (University of South Australia), see: https://lo.unisa.edu.au/course/view.php?id= 6751&sectionid=112501

Godfrey, J. (2014). *Reading and making notes* (2nd edition). Palgrave.

References

Burrell, A. & Tonkin, M. (Eds.). (2020). *Property Crime: Criminological and Psychological Perspectives*. Routledge.

University of South Australia (n.d.). *Exemplary Academic Integrity Project: Resources on academic integrity*. https://lo.unisa.edu.au/course/view.php?id=6751&sectionid= 112507

Williams, K., & Davis, M. (2017). *Referencing and understanding plagiarism* (2nd edition). Palgrave.

Activity 8.1: Answers

Example 1

What the original says	What the student writes	Is this plagiarism?
Successful crime linkage can increase the quantity and quality of evidence available to the police (Ashmore-Hills et al., 2017), which increases the likelihood of apprehending and successfully prosecuting repeat offenders (Grubin et al., 2001).	Successful crime linkage can increase the quantity and quality of evidence available to the police (Ashmore-Hills et al., 2017), which increases the likelihood of apprehending and successfully prosecuting repeat offenders (Grubin et al., 2001).	Yes! It matches word for word

Example 2

What the original says	What the student writes	Is this plagiarism?
Successful crime linkage can increase the quantity and quality of evidence available to the police (Ashmore-Hills et al., 2017), which increases the likelihood of apprehending and successfully prosecuting repeat offenders (Grubin et al., 2001).	Crime linkage can **boost** the quality and quantity of evidence available to **law enforcement** (Ashmore-Hills et al., 2017), which upsurges the prospect of **catching** and successfully prosecuting repeat **criminals** (Grubin et al., 2001).	Yes! • **Changing words is not paraphrasing** • Neither is swapping words over • I've clearly used a thesaurus here • Note the structure of the paragraph is the same as in the original • I have used the same references as the original source (these should be cited as secondary unless I accessed the originals) • I have not cited the original source

Example 3

What the original says	What the student writes	Is this plagiarism?
Successful crime linkage can increase the quantity and quality of evidence available to the police (Ashmore-Hills et al., 2017), which increases the likelihood of apprehending and successfully prosecuting repeat offenders (Grubin et al., 2001).	Crime linkage can be used to support law enforcement to capture and prosecute repeat offenders. This is achieved through an improvement in the amount of good quality evidence identified in serial cases (Burrell & Tonkin, 2020).	No. I have read and understood the key points made by the source and written this in my own words. I have ensured I have cited the primary source I used

Activity 8.2: Answers

Activity	Acceptable or not?
Working in the library together	Yes
Lending someone an assignment	No
Testing each other (e.g. exam revision)	Yes
Asking someone to help you write an assignment	No
Borrowing an assignment	No
Discussing lectures with peers	Yes
Uploading your assignment to an essay-sharing website	No
Sharing references/papers with peers	Yes
Discussing feedback	Yes
Using someone else's assignment as the basis for your own	No
Group work where you have explicitly been told to produce a single, joint report	Yes
Writing joint notes with a peer that would be the basis for an assignment (e.g. content and structure)	No
Sharing memory sticks with peers	No. This might give them access to your work

Activity 8.3: Example answers

There are lots of things you can do to help you avoid plagiarism and collusion. For example:

* Get into good habits
* Don't copy/paste text from original sources into your own notes
* Take the time to digest what you are reading, then make notes
* Include references to support your arguments
* Don't ask to see other students' assignments
* Don't show other students your work
* If you work with others, make sure you each make your own notes and you write up work independently
* Ask your tutor questions if you are unsure of assignment expectations
* Make sure you understand what you are writing about
* Ensure you reference appropriately in the text
* Don't pay someone else to write your essay

Note: This chapter is adapted from learning materials originally developed by Amy Burrell.

9 Critical thinking

Our key aim in this chapter is to explain what critical thinking is and why it is important. We link this directly to University success, as critical thinking is essential for really understanding core research and theory. This understanding, combined with being able to explain and evidence-base your critique, will have a positive impact on your grades. We will provide some good and not so good examples of critical evaluation, and link this to professionalism (e.g. how critical thinking can enhance your career options). The chapter will include some practical tips and exercises to help you develop your critical thinking skills (e.g. questions to ask yourself, how to interpret feedback), with a focus on moving beyond identifying a problem (e.g. small sample) to understanding and explaining why this is an issue for the research (e.g. the sample is not representative/too small to make generalisations from).

Overview of topics

- What is critical thinking?
- Why is critical thinking important for my degree?
- How do I do it?!!
- How do I evidence-base it?
- Supporting others to think critically

Learning outcomes

1 To understand what critical thinking is and why it is important in your Psychology degree
2 To have an opportunity to practise your critical thinking skills

---

What is critical thinking?

Critical thinking is the objective analysis and evaluation of information to make a judgement. It is goal-directed and should be something you do purposefully (i.e. you actively engage in it) so you can make an *informed* judgement.

In summary, it is making decisions based on the best way to think (i.e. avoiding bias). So, rather than choosing an answer because it feels right, the critical thinker will (1) identify all available options and (2) scrutinise each in turn. They will (3) eliminate unreliable information, (4) assess the quality of evidence, and (5) make a judgement based on the best available data.

Why is critical thinking important for my degree?

Critical thinking is important in everyday life, especially for decision-making, and making decisions can be very important (like 'who do I vote for', 'should I marry this person', 'should I move to this new place for a job', 'should I get another dog/cat'...etc.). But why is it so crucial for your degree? Well, we'll tell you why … the better you are at it, the better grades you will get. It's that simple. Students who are good at critical thinking and communicating this do really well. Think of it this way – you can't communicate clearly if your thinking is unclear, and if you can't communicate effectively it will be hard to get good grades. You not only need to be able to identify critical thinking skills, but also how to use them and when to apply them in different circumstances. You don't just want to do well at essays, you also want to demonstrate critical thinking in class activities, work placements, and so on.

Critical thinking is a life skill and the more you practise, the better you will be at it. Let's take your dissertation as an example. If you can think critically, you will be able to answer what we call the 'so, what?' question. This is a hypothetical critical question to ask yourself about your research idea. This means thinking critically about why your research is necessary and what it will achieve. For example, if you are interested in young people's experiences of social media, how would you go about researching this? What would the research tell you? How could it change behaviour for the better? Being able to think critically from the outset will help you determine whether the project is worthwhile in the first place, and if it is, what you might need to consider (e.g. if you want the views of people from a minority group, how will you recruit them?).

Okay, so how do you get started? First, it is easy to think about being critical as finding fault with something. But it is far more than this: it means looking for the strengths/positives as well. Think of it this way – if you don't look at both sides of an argument, how can you make a fully informed judgement? So, being critical at University means being thoughtful, asking questions, not taking things at face value, finding information and understanding different approaches, and then using this in your writing.

Oh, and one last thing … employers want to take on people who are critical thinkers! Think about it – would you rather employ someone who can use their critical thinking skills to work on finding a solution to a problem or someone who is passive, is illogical in their approach, and/or whose thinking/communication is unclear?

How do I do it?!!

Everyone thinks they are doing critical thinking but if you can't explain what you are doing, you might not actually be doing it. We also tend to think that things are right or wrong – the so-called black or white approach. In reality there are many shades of grey (especially when studying human behaviour!) and critical thinking helps us identify what these are and what they mean.

A good example of critical thinking is recognising the difference between a correlation and cause-and-effect:

> **Correlation** refers to the relationship between two factors (variables) – this can be positive or negative.
>
> **Cause-and-effect** – or causation/causality – is where one factor (variable) has a *direct* influence on another factor (variable).

However, people often use the terms interchangeably when they really shouldn't. Let's take an example: increases in ice cream sales are associated with an increase in shark attacks (see Figure 9.1).

Is this correlation or causation? Just because two things co-occur does not mean that they are connected. I think we can agree that this is correlation (unless sharks are only targeting people eating ice cream!). Without further information we could never say that increases in ice cream sales *cause* shark attacks and yet these kinds of spurious connections are made between variables in research and presented as causation. In this example, it is far more likely that another factor (or extraneous variable) is impacting on these two outcomes. For example, we could test if these increases are associated with hot weather. In this case, eating more ice cream or spending more time in the sea (which may increase your risk of being attacked by a shark) is more understandable. It may be that the hot weather also leads to other trends, such as an increase in the sale of sunglasses or a decrease in the spread of a virus. Now we have considered the mechanism for why relationships might exist between our variables, we have begun to develop our hypotheses: e.g. hot weather may cause an increase in ice cream sales, etc. (see Figure 9.2). This is something we can then test – with the appropriate methods and statistical analyses of course! (see Chapter 6).

Figure 9.1 Ice cream vs. sharks

  =

Increase in ice cream sales   Increase in shark attacks

Figure 9.2 Sun vs. ice cream, sharks, sunglasses, and viral spread

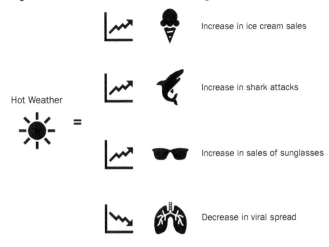

So, correlation is what we call a 'logical fallacy' – i.e. the reasoning may appear logical when in fact it is not. It is important to avoid this trap, such as when reports in the media present correlation as causation. This is why you need to be able to discern between correlation and causation and apply this in your real-life interpretation of data. Understanding the difference also helps you unpick findings. For example, if children who go to pre-school read better than their peers who don't, does that mean attending pre-school is the cause, or is it because wealthier kids go to pre-school and something else in their background gives them an advantage?

We also need to consider how to avoid bias. There are many different types of bias (we recommend Practical Psychology, 2016, for a good summary) but here we'll take hindsight bias as our example. Hindsight bias is the human tendency to overestimate our ability to have predicted an outcome after the fact. This is where you'll hear people confidently claim, 'I knew it!', or that they predicted their team would win the local derby. Even if they did suggest the outcome, their confidence in their pre-outcome decision-making will grow. So, you'll hear people say, 'I think my team will win', but after the game the narrative will switch to 'I knew they would win, I predicted it' – this is hindsight bias. We commonly see this in write-ups of research when students 'adjust' or 'amend' their hypotheses to match their findings. This is bad practice. What you need to do is build an evidence-based rationale for why you made the prediction you did. It may be that upon analysing the results you realise why your research didn't achieve the outcome you predicted. Well, that's okay. Rejecting a well-formulated, evidence-based hypothesis with a robust analysis is a perfectly legitimate outcome for research. If you do have some hindsight as to why, great – write that up in your discussion. Don't change your hypotheses.

Okay, now for some practical tips about how to engage in critical thinking.

The most common mistake that students make in critical analysis is simply to make a list of limitations/gaps, when it is important to weigh up both the strengths and weaknesses of research evidence/theory. Furthermore, when you identify a strength or limitation, tell the reader *why* this is important. We are often told something vague like, 'oh, but the sample was small', rather than being given an explanation as to *why* this was an issue, what impact it might have had on the interpretation of findings, and how these might be used in practice.

Remember, there are different levels of criticism from the very general to the very specific (see Figure 9.3). The *general* limitations of a study might include a small sample size, the sample not being generalisable (e.g. the participants were all female Psychology students, so the results are not generalisable to the population as a whole), unreliable self-report data, lack of ecological validity of a laboratory study, and so on.

Being more *specific* means explaining, for example, why a small sample led to a lack of statistical power, and why your self-report data might be unreliable.

For a top grade, you need to explain how to avoid a problem you encountered in the future. For example, if you recruited many more female than male participants, this might have skewed the results (explain how!), and future research should aim for a more equal gender balance. The following is a real example from a published piece of research. Waldeck et al. (2017) found that psychological flexibility was a moderator of the distress associated with perceived ostracism. However, the authors noted that there were not many males in the sample. As such, the findings could arguably have limited application to males as there was not enough statistical power to detect effects between the sexes. This is important because the literature is generally mixed in regard to sex differences – some studies show that males are more affected by ostracism, others show that females are. The authors in this case suggested that future research should aim to include more male participants where possible, but also defended their results, since they ran additional analyses to rule out sex as a critical factor. They also provided a theoretical argument to suggest that such individual differences should not matter, as everyone is impacted by ostracism equally (i.e. it is automatically painful whoever you are), at least in the short term.

Figure 9.3 Levels of criticism

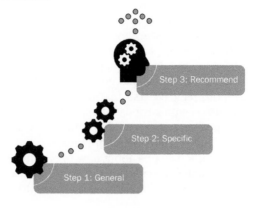

Thus, although addressing the general and specific limitations of a study is important, it is when you state what needs to be done to avoid similar problems in the future that you are really demonstrating the depth of your critique. Unfortunately, many students only address general limitations, which usually results in a partial critique or weak arguments. Take ecological validity, for example. Some students are happy to say, 'oh, it's a lab study, therefore there is no ecological validity'. Mm, okay, but is that it? Others might even tell you that the study lacks ecological validity because the findings aren't generalisable. Better, but still vague. What you need to do is explain *why* a laboratory experiment might generate non-generalisable results.

One way to do this is to compare laboratory conditions with a specific real-world context to see how comparable they are (or not) and then build an argument around this. For example, take the Bobo Doll experiment (Bandura et al., 1961) in which children witnessed an adult hitting a doll. The children then later mimicked that behaviour. But does this mean children would mimic an adult in a different context? Say, an adult they saw on TV – would they copy what they saw on TV? If so, why? If not, why not? There is a difference between seeing aggressive behaviour in real life versus on-screen, so you cannot infer that aggression in the lab would extend to other contexts. Also, in the Bobo Doll experiment children displayed their aggression in the same environment in which they saw aggression happen. When watching violence on TV in real life, it is unlikely they would come across the exact same situation they saw on screen. This is not to say the results of this experiment have no value (indeed, it was ground-breaking at the time) but instead that we should be aware of how far the findings can actually be applied to a real-world setting. Bandura and his colleagues conducted a lot more research on aggression (including media influences), so, if you are interested in the topic, it is worth looking up his work.

You should also consider the wider context, such as when a study was published (is it out of date?), where it was conducted (are the results transferable to other contexts/cultures?), and who published it (is the evidence being presented coming from the academic who proposed the theory in the first place?). Furthermore, it will be important to know who funded the research. For example, if the drug company whose drug is being tested funded the work, this could result in publication bias (i.e. only publishing results that show the drug works). To help you do this for yourself, we recommend 5 bums on a bench!

Questions to ask yourself – 5 bums on a bench!

There are questions you should ask yourself when critiquing anything. You will see this referred to as the 5Ws and 1H as a way to structure critical thinking (e.g. Vertes & Ste-Marie, 2012; Waisbord, 2019). This refers to Who, What, Why, When, Where, and How and can be used to help us ask critical questions. 5Ws and 1H is a bit boring though, so we prefer to call this the 5 bums on a bench. Let us explain. When thinking about critiquing a piece of research, ask yourself the questions in Figure 9.4.

Students tend to do the 'how' and give a good summary of any issues with the methods (e.g. sample size). Sometimes they consider the 'where' (e.g. the

Figure 9.4 5 bums on a bench

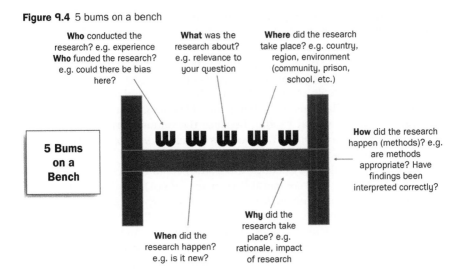

Who conducted the research? e.g. experience
Who funded the research? e.g. could there be bias here?

What was the research about? e.g. relevance to your question

Where did the research take place? e.g. country, region, environment (community, prison, school, etc.)

5 Bums on a Bench

How did the research happen (methods)? e.g. are methods appropriate? Have findings been interpreted correctly?

When did the research happen? e.g. is it new?

Why did the research take place? e.g. rationale, impact of research

research was conducted abroad and so not generalisable to a UK population) but their offering tends to be rather limited. We believe the 'where' should also include things like where it was published. For example, an article published in a high-impact journal will carry more weight than a paper that has not been peer-reviewed. The other bums meanwhile are often forgotten, even though they can add so much to your critique!

The first thing you should consider, for example, is the 'what' – in the sense that you need to know whether the research you are reading is relevant to what you want to write about. If not, bin it straightaway! The 'why' is also super-useful – for example, was there a good rationale for the research? If not, don't consider it further. Also, was there an impact value to the research? Is it close enough to real life to inform practice (e.g. adapt a crime prevention intervention, develop a new treatment, inform development or update of theory)? If not, this could be critiqued. Then there is the 'when' – when did the research happen? If it was conducted 20 years ago, can we be confident the findings remain applicable? Finally, and the most forgotten, is the 'who'. For example, what is the expertise of the person doing the research? You should also consider the broader picture – for example, is all the evidence for the theory you are writing about restricted to the same researcher(s), or even the person who proposed the theory in the first place? Is that offender management programme being evaluated by the people who designed it? Lots of scope for potential bias there. This is not to say researchers are biased but it is worth considering if the research is as objective as it could be. There would be stronger supporting evidence, for example, if different groups of researchers also report the same outcomes. 'Who' might also include who funded the research – do they have a vested interest in the outcome? This could be a pharmaceutical company looking for evidence that their very expensive drug is effective. Again, this is not to say the research is definitely biased but you would require independent evidence to back up any claims made in papers sponsored by someone with a vested interest. A good question to ask yourself when considering the 'who' is 'who benefits?' – who will benefit from a particular piece of research and how the findings are interpreted? Let's look at a real example.

In 1998, Wakefield and colleagues published a paper in *The Lancet* (a highly respected medical journal) indicating a link between the measles, mumps, and rubella (MMR) vaccine and developmental disorders in children. This directly resulted in a drop in vaccine uptake (Sathyanarayana Rao & Andrade, 2011). Despite extensive concerns about the research (including the small, selective sample of 12 participants and ethics violations), retraction of the paper by *The Lancet*, and a number of more robust studies refuting the authors' claims (e.g. Taylor et al., 1999), the so-called link between the MMR vaccine and autism is still having an impact on vaccine uptake today (Belluz, 2019). Why might this be the case? Who might have benefited from the authors' interpretation of the findings? Well, it has since been established that Wakefield and his colleagues had financial links to people who would have wanted to see this particular outcome, namely lawyers for parents who were suing vaccine companies (Sathyanarayana Rao & Andrade, 2011). Thus, it was in their interests that the study came to a particular conclusion, and there is evidence that the authors manipulated the data to get the outcome they wanted (Godlee, 2011). The question remains, however, why do some people continue to believe there is a link? There are a number of reasons for this, including that the issue is highly emotive and, combined with a lack of medical knowledge and/or clear understanding of risk, some people are more risk-averse and will avoid the vaccine, 'just in case'. Or, it could be linked to a lack of balanced reporting – for example, a vaccine scare sells more newspapers than a story about the benefits of vaccines. Interestingly, the retraction of the 1998 paper commanded a small, anonymous paragraph in the *The Lancet* (Sathyanarayana Rao & Andrade, 2011).

More tips:

1 Get into the habit of reading – this will provide you with examples of good critiquing skills.

2 Make sure you attend class and engage in learning – another way of learning good critiquing skills.

3 If you don't know where to start, focus on things the researcher can control for (i.e. strengths) and things they can't (i.e. limitations).

4 Critical thinking is not just repeating another person's critique. We hear you say, 'but I was told to evidence-base my critique!' Yes, that's right, but the evidence on which you base your critique doesn't necessarily have to come from your topic area. For example, if you critique the methods of a study and find there is an issue, this part of your argument might be supported by the research methods literature. Don't exaggerate your claims though – there is a difference between the superficial identification of a limitation in a single paper and the integrated, in-depth critical evaluation of an area of research as a whole. Basically, don't claim that a whole research area needs to change based on the outcomes/methods/critique of a single paper.

5   Apply what you have learned to *your* study/assignment. For example, if you are building a rationale for your dissertation project, how does the paper you have just read help you do that?

6   Remember there is no limit to the number of critical points you make. We often get asked, 'how many are you looking for?', as if there were a magic number! Here is how Amy recently responded in relation to a case study assignment: 'This is a bit like asking "how long is a piece of string?", as it depends on lots of factors (e.g. which theory you are discussing, how much literature there is on that theory, which behaviour this relates to in the case, etc.). I would expect to see multiple points of critique for any theory you discuss. Remember that critique includes strengths and limitations. The more points of critique you have, the better chance of a higher grade. There is no upper limit. I would hope the assignment would contain critique throughout'. Chances are you will get a similar answer regardless of which tutor you ask or which assignment the question relates to!

7   Take care when writing up – your aim is not to antagonise people whose work you are critiquing. You need to pitch this appropriately – remember you might come across these people at a later date. People are fine with constructive critique but not character assassination!

8   Use free resources – see, for example, Thematic Education's (2019) video on '3 steps to evaluate a study'.

Okay, now you have considered what questions to ask, you need to evidence-base your critique. But how?

How do I evidence-base it?

You will need to provide citations/references to support your critique, which need to be of good quality (see Chapter 7 for a discussion of types of evidence). There are a few additional tips that are particularly helpful when sourcing evidence for critical points though. Here goes:

*   Remember, finding evidence/studies to support your arguments is part of critical thinking, as you are identifying which sources are the most appropriate (i.e. good quality). You will receive credit for the quality of your evidence.

*   A lack of supporting evidence (e.g. for a theory) might be something you need to critique. If you can't find anything to support an argument, this likely signals that there is a lack of research in the area. Make sure, however, that you provide supporting evidence for a lack of research! We have lost count of how many times we have been told there is 'literally no research on this' only to find a quick Google search results in hundreds of hits!

*   Think about how recent your evidence is. Your tutors will encourage you to use up-to-date literature to evidence-base your arguments. Having said this, however, you can't help when a theory was proposed, so we would expect to

see older references in relation to this! However, if you are critiquing theory using literature that is so old that it is impacting on the strength of your argument (e.g. you argue there is no recent research when there clearly is – see previous point!), then this would be a problem.

- Check for assumptions and personal views – make sure your evidence is presented objectively and supported with evidence (i.e. references).
- Check sweeping statements and generalisations. For instance, something might be true in one context but not another, so make sure your assertion is appropriate based on the evidence you present.

Supporting others to think critically

We also recommend thinking about how you can support others to think critically. The most obvious example is how you provide feedback. For example, if you are asked to give peer feedback, what should it look like? Remember, being critical is not just about highlighting problems. Being critical means offering a critique, so make sure you highlight their strengths as well. Think also about the language you use – would you prefer to be told that your evidence-base could be stronger or that your evidence-base is crap? Another tip is to say how they could strengthen their work. Don't just tell them what's wrong but instead offer advice on how it could be improved. Similarly, if their work was good, why was it good? This will help them to replicate their strengths in their next piece of work. (See Chapter 5 for more about feedback).

Talking point: we are not all critical in the same way

Let's do some myth-busting. Students think that their tutors have an 'answer sheet' for essays. This simply isn't the case. We ask you a question and then look for you to build and make your argument. We do have marking schemes but these centre on content insofar as whether it is relevant to the topic under discussion. Much more of your credit is awarded for critical evaluation (i.e. how well you make an argument) and evidence (i.e. how well you evidence-base your argument). Thus, different students will come up with different answers to the same question. This is fine, so long as you all answer the question. Here is an example from Amy, who used to work for a security training company. Students asked to argue what the main purpose of security management was became fixated on finding the correct answer. Amy's response? – 'I don't mind what you choose so long as you build an argument and evidence-base it. You can tell me the main purpose of security management is to paint the sky purple with pink spots. If you make a robust argument for this (unlikely but you never know!) and evidence-base it you will do well!' You are Psychologists now – there **is no right answer**, only a well-argued, evidence-based one.

Take home message

1 Don't confuse correlation with causation.
2 Remember to explain *why* things are a problem (e.g. just saying sample size is too small = grr!).
3 Apply what you have learned to *your* study/assignment.
4 Evidence-base everything!

Activity 9.1: Looking at both sides of something

This activity is designed to help you practise thinking critically. Look at the examples below and try to build a robust argument for *and* against each. Feel free to use the internet or other sources to read around the topics to help you with the activity.

Example 1: The death penalty

The death penalty is the state-sanctioned killing of a person as punishment for a crime. For example, in the USA a conviction for murder could result in the death penalty, most likely execution by lethal injection. What are the possible arguments for and against the death penalty?

Arguments for the death penalty	Arguments against the death penalty

Example 2: Positive discrimination

Some companies lack diversity in their workforce. One possible way of increasing diversity is to introduce a policy of positive discrimination (e.g. people with certain characteristics – whether based on gender, ethnicity, or disability – are guaranteed an interview). What are the possible arguments for and against such an approach?

Arguments for positive discrimination	Arguments against positive discrimination

Activity 9.2: Do you question the reliability of the news? If so, why? What tactics do you use? Perhaps think about a particular news story you doubted to help you get started. Write these down in the box below – you might find them useful when critiquing academic literature!

Chapter resources

Amnesty International (2017). *The death penalty and deterrence.* https://www.amnesty-usa.org/issues/death-penalty/death-penalty-facts/the-death-penalty-and-deterrence/

Death Penalty Information Center: https://deathpenaltyinfo.org/

Godfrey, J. (2016). *Writing for university* (2nd edition). Palgrave.

Practical Psychology (2021). *Self-fulfilling prophecy (definition + examples).* [Video] YouTube, 22 March. https://www.youtube.com/watch?v=hy7CptLHiV0

Practical Psychology (2016, December 30). *12 cognitive biases explained – How to think better and more logically removing bias.* [Video] YouTube, 30 December. https://www.youtube.com/watch?v=wEwGBIr_RIw

Thematic Education (2019). *Evaluate any study in 3 simple steps.* [Video] YouTube, 13 November. https://www.youtube.com/watch?v=YUTkqRknNok

Williams, K. (2014). *Getting critical* (2nd edition). Palgrave.

References

Bandura, A., Ross, D., & Ross, S. (1961). Transmission of aggression through imitation of aggressive models. *Journal of Abnormal and Social Psychology, 63*(3), 575–582. https://doi.org/10.1037/h0045925

Belluz, J. (2019). *Research fraud cataylzed the anti-vaccination movement: Let's not repeat history.* https://www.vox.com/2018/2/27/17057990/andrew-wakefield-vaccines-autism-study

Godlee, F. (2011). The fraud behind the MMR scare. *British Medical Journal, 342*, d22. https://doi.org/10.1136/bmj.d22

Sathyanarayana Rao, T.S., & Andrade, C. (2011). The MMR vaccine and autism: sensation, refutation, retraction, and fraud. *Indian Journal of Psychiatry, 53*(2), 95–96. https://doi.org/10.4103/0019-5545.82529

Taylor, B., Miller, E., Farrington, C.P., Petropoulos, M.C., Favot-Mayaud, I., Li, J. et al. (1999). Autism and measles, mumps, and rubella vaccine: no epidemiological evidence for causal association. *Lancet, 353*(9169), 2026–2029. https://doi.org/10.1016/s0140-6736(99)01239-8

Vertes, K.A., & Ste-Marie, D.M. (2012). Trampolinists' self-controlled use of a feedforward self-modelling video in competition. *Journal of Applied Sport Psychology, 25*(4), 463–477. https://doi.org/10.1080/10413200.2012.756705

Waisbord, S. (2019). The 5Ws and 1H of digital journalism. *Digital Journalism, 7*(3), 351–358. https://doi.org/10.1080/21670811.2018.1545592

Wakefield, A.J., Murch, S.H., Anthony, A., Linnell, J., Casson, D.M., Malik, M. et al. (1998). Illeal-lymphoid-modular hyperplasia, non-specific colitis, and pervasive developmental disorder in children. *Lancet, 351*(9103), 637–641. https://doi.org/10.1016/s0140-6736(97)11096-0

Waldeck, D., Tyndall, I., Riva, P., & Chmiel, N. (2017). How do we cope with ostracism? Psychological flexibility moderates the relationship between everyday ostracism experiences and psychological distress. *Journal of Contextual Behavioral Science, 6*(4), 425–432.

Activity 9.1: Example answers

Example 1: The death penalty

Arguments for the death penalty	Arguments against the death penalty
• Acts as a punishment • Closure for families of victims • Offender cannot commit more violent offences (thus preventing further victims) • Community feels safer	• Offenders are still people and have human rights • Lack of opportunity for rehabilitation • It is expensive to keep offenders on death row (e.g. cost of appeals) • The death penalty does not deter offenders (data from the Death Penalty Information Center shows that US states with the death penalty have higher murder rates per 100,000 population)

Example 2: Positive discrimination

Arguments for positive discrimination	Arguments against positive discrimination
• Can help quickly boost diversity within a team/ workplace • Widens opportunities for disadvantaged populations/ candidates	• Could mean people are recruited on the basis of their characteristics rather than because they are best qualified to do the job • Could mean good candidates who don't have a particular characteristic will miss out on the opportunity • There are other ways diversity could be boosted – e.g. removing age, gender, ethnicity from application forms so that employers are less prone to using unconscious bias when making interview shortlist selections

Activity 9.2: Example answer

Hopefully you have said 'yes', you do question what you read/hear in the news! It is useful to have a questioning mindset when reading news articles – this can help you identify sources of information that help you make a judgement about veracity (i.e. how truthful it is). Considering the source is one tactic you might have identified you use – for example, is the newspaper independent of political influence, does it lean to the left/right (as that will influence how they frame stories). Second, who is the author of the article? If they quote facts and statistics, do they tell you where they got them from? The Office for National Statistics, for example, would be a reliable source of statistics. Bear in mind though that a news article might only tell you part of the story (i.e. interpret statistics to suit its needs!) – what are they not telling you?

10 What next?

This is the final chapter of the book, which will round off what we have talked about and highlight the key messages we have discussed. Moreover, we will give you some pointers about what you can do before starting your course. We'll also highlight where you can find interesting and useful resources, such as the BPS website, job websites, blogs, and so on. Additionally, there are some activities for you to do to get started – for example, putting together your personal development plan, building relationships with personal tutors, identifying where the careers service is located, and booking appointments with support services who offer skills classes on topics such as writing skills and how to reference correctly.

Overview of topics

- Summary of key messages
- How to prepare for your course
- SWOT analysis
- SMART goals
- Final words!

Learning outcome

1 To identify an action plan for your Psychology degree and beyond

Summary of key messages

Throughout each chapter you have been introduced to key messages (e.g. the need to act professionally, the need to be an independent learner, the need to reflect continuously on your development, etc.). To help remind yourself of these key messages, copy the diagram (Figure 10.1) on the next page and stick it on your wall (or maybe use it as a screensaver on your phone [ok, perhaps not this option, but you get the idea!]). It can certainly be useful to have a visual reminder which you can come to and remind yourself of how you can succeed in your Psychology degree.

Figure 10.1 Key messages

How to prepare for your course

Well … you have got off to a good start by reading this book to help you make the most out of your Psychology degree! However, it is also a good idea to do some additional reading to introduce you to some of the core domains and topics covered in Psychology. It is hard to recommend a single book/resource but here are some good places to start. Students might be interested in some or all of the reading below regardless of the course they wish to follow.

Gross, R. (2020). *The psychology of mind and behaviour* (8th ed.). Hodder Education. This is a good all-round Psychology book.

Howitt, D. (2018). *Introduction to forensic and criminal psychology* (6th ed.). Pearson. This will be of most interest to Forensic/Criminal Psychology students but all psychology students might wish to read this (especially if you do a module on the topic).

Weinberg, R., & Gould, D. (2018). *Foundations of sport and exercise psychology* (7th ed.). Champaign, IL: Human Kinetics. This will be of most interest to students studying Sport and Exercise Psychology.

You don't have to buy textbooks to get a head start with your reading. Your University library will have similar resources available to read as soon as you arrive. If you want to start with free resources, take a look at the below. The most important thing is to start reading – where you start is up to you!

- The British Psychological Society publishes a magazine called *The Psychologist* (see https://thepsychologist.bps.org.uk/). This is not a formal academic source (i.e. we wouldn't expect you to quote it in assignments) but it is a good place to keep up to date with what is new in Psychology.

- Lots of academic journals provide sample issues or have open access papers you can read; for example, the *British Journal of Psychology* has a free sample issue on its website (see https://onlinelibrary.wiley.com/toc/10.1111/ (ISSN)2044-8295/free-sample). This will allow you to access academic papers for free to start your reading. If you see journal papers you are interested in but can't access, make a note of them and look them up when you start your course!

Other ideas for reading

TopUniversities.com also has an interesting recommended reading list for Psychology students at https://www.topuniversities.com/courses/psychology/8-books-read-if-youre-psychology-student. There are what appear to be odd choices included here but there are some really good reads. The *Little book of psychology* by Emily Ralls and Caroline Riggs is a good choice for those of you new to Psychology.

You might also be interested in study guides, a lot of which are on the market (and in your University library!). Pocket guides are particularly useful and cover a range of topics, including:

- Writing for University
- Planning your Essay
- Reflective Writing
- Reading and Making Notes
- Getting Critical
- Using Feedback to Boost Your Grades
- Referencing and Understanding Plagiarism
- Where's Your Evidence?
- Studying with Dyslexia
- Managing Stress

See https://www.macmillanihe.com/series/Pocket-Study-Skills/14549/ for more information.

Moreover, relevant magazines such as *The Psychologist* (mentioned above) and websites like that of the APA (e.g. https://www.apa.org/news) will introduce you to current hot topics in Psychology. This will help you to understand how Psychology is applied to current events. Keep track of such resources – they might potentially steer you in the right direction for a dissertation topic later on in your degree!

SWOT analysis

Now that you are aware of what to expect from your degree, it is a good time to consider ... *what next?* Throughout your degree, different University staff (particularly your personal tutor [or equivalent]) will advise you to think about creating an action plan to ensure you keep developing professionally. However, before you develop your action plan, it is useful to do a SWOT analysis. This involves identifying your **S**trengths, **W**eaknesses, **O**pportunities, and **T**hreats. A SWOT can help you to understand your weaknesses, recognise any opportunities to help you grow (which you may have missed), and acknowledge threats to your learning which you can then manage and minimise.

Here are a couple of handy resources to help you prepare for writing for your SWOT analysis:

https://www.getmyuni.com/articles/swot-analysis-for-students
https://blog.capterra.com/s-w-o-t-analysis-examples-for-beginners/

And here are also some key questions to consider when completing each section of the SWOT analysis:

Strengths

- What advantages do you have that others do not (e.g. specific skills, education, work experience, connections to industry)?
- What do you do better than others? (e.g. Do you think more critically? Are you better at Maths/Statistics? More organised? More confident in communication?)
- What do others (e.g. your tutors, peers, work colleagues, employers) see as your strengths?

Weaknesses

- Do you have any traits which could impact on your academic performance (e.g. fearing public speaking)?
- Are you disorganised (e.g. tend to miss or be unprepared for deadlines)?
- Do you procrastinate (e.g. watch a video on YouTube during your dedicated writing time)?
- Do you struggle to manage stress?
- Where have you been marked down on previous assignments?

Opportunities

- Do you have any contacts or people in your network who you call upon for support or guidance?
- Are there any conferences you can attend? Any University facilities, societies, or clubs to help you learn?

Threats

- What obstacles do you face at work/home?
- Do you/will you have competing demands (e.g. childcare, work commitments)?
- Is there anything that could threaten your personal or professional development?

Now let's look at what a completed SWOT might look like. Imagine a student is starting their Psychology degree. They might write the following:

Strengths

* I am really motivated and passionate about Psychology.

Weaknesses

* I tend to struggle to concentrate for long periods and often procrastinate (e.g. play on Xbox when I should be working).
* I have difficulties organising my time.
* I am often nervous of speaking in front of other people.

Opportunities

* There are some non-academic opportunities to develop skills, e.g. joining a sports team will help me learn teamwork and make me more confident working with others.
* I can get support from my Careers Service to gain relevant work experience.
* I can book a meeting with my personal tutor (or equivalent) for support and guidance.

Threats

* I have two young children who I care for.
* It can be a challenge balancing paid work and University work.

Activity 10.1: Time to SWOT up!

Now that you have seen an example of a SWOT, have a go at writing your own SWOT analysis. Use the template provided.

SWOT ANALYSIS	
MY STRENGTHS (S)	**MY WEAKNESSES (W)**
MY OPPORTUNITIES (O)	**MY THREATS (T)**

Now that you have completed your SWOT, this can help form the foundation of your action plan. Why do you need an action plan? Well, it can help you turn your weaknesses into strengths. And it can help you create a timescale for when you will do specific actions (e.g. take available opportunities, minimise threats) to further your personal and/or professional development. For example, if you fear public speaking (which may impact on presentation assignments), you may take the opportunity to slowly develop your confidence and practise your public speaking in a safe environment, such as by joining a club or society. Action plans can be really helpful whatever the stage of your course or career. For example, if you are just starting out, you could create a plan focusing on ensuring you are as prepared for the course as possible (such as attending orientation/induction). If creating an action plan during your course, it might focus on how you can develop following specific feedback on one of your assignments, or to prepare for obtaining relevant work experience. Or, you could put in place a plan to help you prepare for when you have finished your degree (e.g. prepare for job interviews, apply for postgraduate courses).

Whatever stage you are at, it is also a good idea to identify what barriers are preventing you from succeeding, and plan to overcome these obstacles. In our experience, this is what students tend to struggle with most. Indeed, in reflection-based assignments, students often get lower marks when it comes to developing their action plan because they are unable to specify their plans clearly (e.g. 'I will work on this') or they are unrealistic (e.g. 'I have failed my statistics assignment. I will read a statistics textbook every day until I understand'). It would be more appropriate in this instance to plan to speak to the marker of the assignment to clarify anything regarding the feedback you were unclear about. And one way of developing a solid action plan is to adopt SMART goals.

SMART goals

Do you remember what we mean by SMART goals, which we touched on in Chapter 5? SMART is an acronym that you can use to guide your own goal-setting. To help make sure your goals are achievable and sufficiently clear, they need to be: **S**pecific, **M**easurable, **A**chievable, **R**ealistic, and **T**imebound.

Specific: State what *exactly* you want to achieve – whether in your academic/professional life or personal life. If your goals are vague, it will be difficult for you to achieve anything. Include clear details that explain the what, why, who, where, and when of a goal.

Measurable: It is important you have an objective means of tracking and measuring your progress. Otherwise, how will you know you have achieved your goal?

Achievable: Your goal must be attainable. Do you have the skills required to achieve a particular goal? If so, what are they? If not, what additional support or training would you need?

Realistic: It is important that your goal challenges you, but it also needs to be relevant. Consider questions such as: Does it seem worthwhile? Will it actually contribute to my development? Is it feasible? Is the timeframe I am proposing realistic?

Timebound: Your goal needs to have a deadline. When will you actually achieve your goal? It can be helpful to put in place some milestones (i.e. mini targets) to help you gauge your progress: What can I do today, in a month's time, in six months' time to achieve my goal?

Okay, now you know what SMART goals are, let's consider a couple of examples of bad and good SMART goals (see Table 10.1).

Table 10.1   Good and bad SMART goals

Example of a Bad SMART goal	What needs to be improved to make it better?	Example of a Good SMART goal
I want to buy a house	• Is it realistic? (e.g. if juggling other costs and commitments such as childcare and full-time study, is now the right time to be saving?) • This goal needs to be *measurable*. For example, how much money do you need to save for the deposit? • It needs to have a clear *deadline* (i.e. *when* will you have saved the money for the deposit, and when do you think you will be able to move in?) • When you have long-term goals, it is useful to have put in place some milestones (i.e. small rewards) to help keep you motivated and on target.	I need to save approximately £18,000 in order to have a deposit to buy a house in the next six years. As I have several other costs to consider (e.g. childcare, bills, tuition), I used a savings calculator on the MoneyAdvice Service Website. I will save £300 every month over the next five years. When I achieve my monthly savings target, I will reward myself (e.g. cook my favourite meal, get a massage, treat myself to a hot bath). *Note: Of course, there are other specific elements to mention in planning to buy a house (e.g. surveying, liaising with solicitors etc.); this is just to give you the idea of a more tangible goal!*

(continued)

Table 10.1 (continued)

Example of a Bad SMART goal	What needs to be improved to make it better?	Example of a Good SMART goal
I want to become a better student	• This is not *specific* enough. Of course you will want to be as good a student as you can be, but does this mean you need to work on how you write academically? Do you need to improve your grades? Are you unable to complete the tasks you are set? Are you missing deadlines? • The goal needs to be *measurable. How will you know* when you are a 'better student'? • *When will you know* you have met your target? You need to set deadlines.	I have received feedback on my last two assignments that my spelling and grammar have been poor. To become better at this, I will book a meeting with my writing support service next week to develop my writing skills. I will also book a meeting with my marker to ask how I could have rephrased some of my sentences correctly. I will review this target after my next essay is marked at the end of the semester to see if I have improved and whether I get fewer comments about spelling and grammar.

As you will see from Table 10.1, to have a tangible goal that is achievable, it is important to ask yourself critical questions (i.e. by adopting the SMART framework). This will give your action plan much more *depth* and allow you to evidence your reflection skills well.

Activity 10.2: Create your own SMART action plan

Now you know what you need to consider when creating an action plan/setting SMART goals, have a go at creating your own SMART action plan. Use the template provided.

Final words!

We hope you have enjoyed reading our book. You will have seen different themes throughout relating to the need to be professional and take responsibility for your learning. In our experience, the best-performing students tend to be those who use their initiative, act professionally (e.g. behave according to the BPS Code of Ethics and Conduct), and, importantly, learn from their feedback and *keep developing*. You have taken a positive step already by reading this book in preparing yourself for a successful degree journey. Similarly, if you engage with planning activities (e.g. SMART goals) on a regular basis, this will help you keep on track and be successful. You can return to any part of this book throughout your degree to refresh your memory on some of our key messages. Finally ... let us leave you to consider a quote from Charles Swindoll:

Life is 10% what happens to you and 90% how you respond to it.

SMART steps	Description
Specific	
Measurable	
Achievable	
Realistic	
Timebound	

Chapter resources

For *The Psychologist* magazine, see: https://thepsychologist.bps.org.uk/

The *British Journal of Psychology* offers **open access/free sample issues**. See: https://onlinelibrary.wiley.com/toc/10.1111/(ISSN)2044-8295/free-sample

TopUniversities has a useful **recommended reading list** for Psychology students. See: https://www.topuniversities.com/courses/psychology/8-books-read-if-youre-psychology-student

For the **Pocket Study Skills** guides, see: https://www.macmillanihe.com/series/Pocket-Study-Skills/14549/

See the APA website for current **hot topics in Psychology**, e.g. https://www.apa.org/news

For useful examples of a **SWOT analysis**, see: https://www.getmyuni.com/articles/swot-analysis-for-students& https://blog.capterra.com/s-w-o-t-analysis-examples-for-beginners/

References

Charles R. Swindoll Quotes, *BrainyQuote* (n.d.). https://www.brainyquote.com/quotes/charles_r_swindoll_388332

Ralls, E., & Riggs, C. (2019). *The little book of psychology: An introduction to the key psychologists and theories you need to know.* Summersdale.

Activity 10.1: Feedback

Strengths, Weaknesses, Opportunities, and Threats will vary from person to person. Think about things in general that will have an influence on you (e.g. moving away from home and beginning life at University), and things that are more particular to you as an individual (e.g. maybe you are a carer and this places limits on your time).

Activity 10.2: Answers

Ideally, you will have followed the SMART goals to ensure that your action plan is sufficiently clear (and has sufficient depth). It's useful to practise with this structure to get used to SMART goals. However, as you become more confident, aim to start writing in prose (e.g. as in Table 10.1) rather than under separate headings. This will help your writing flow and help whoever is reading your action plan (or marking it!) to follow it.

Here are some example SMART goals which you may find useful templates. We provide a weak example and a good example for each:

Context: I am already at University and preparing for a work experience/ job application

Weak example: I want to have some work experience. I will start searching for jobs, but I am quite nervous about the interviews. I am normally quite weak at presenting in front of others.

Good example:

SMART steps	Description
Specific	I want to become confident and perform well at interviews, as I am often very nervous speaking in front of others. I have never had an interview before.
Measurable	I will begin searching for relevant tips on general interview skills by the end of this week. I will also book a meeting with my career development team at the University to help me prepare and give me guidance. I will also ask the staff about how I can improve my CV writing.
Achievable	I am going to practice by video recording myself answering some mock interview questions. I will play it back and write down my strengths and weaknesses, and keep practicing to improve those areas that need developing. I am also going to build my confidence for speaking in front of others by volunteering to speak for my seminar group later this month.
Realistic	Developing my presenting skills will help me to perform well at interview. It will also be helpful in the future as the job market for future Psychology roles will be very competitive.
Timebound	In a month's time I will be more proficient in my interview skills. I will apply for work experience by continuing to engage with the career development team (e.g. helping to shape my cover letter) and aim to have an interview within two months.

Context: I am really scared about starting my Stats module

Weak example: I am quite anxious about statistics and tend to avoid engaging with the activities my tutor sets. I will read a chapter of the statistics book every week so that I understand all the concepts.

Good example:

SMART steps	Description
Specific	I want to become more confident in my ability to do statistics and get a good grade on my Research Methods module.
Measurable	I will book an appointment this week with my personal tutor (or equivalent) to advise me how I can achieve a high grade on this module. I will take heed of their suggestions and devise a plan to work towards this target. I will also note down all the weekly reading materials recommended by my tutor.

SMART steps	Description
Achievable	Tomorrow I will be creating a weekly schedule to help organise and plan my learning. This schedule will include both non-academic (e.g. work hours, social time with friends, sports club training and matches) and academic time (e.g. taught sessions, self-study times, assessment writing). I will make sure that I allocate at least five hours each week to focus specifically on learning and practicing statistics outside of the taught seminar slots. These dates and times will be added to my University Outlook Calendar, which is also installed on my phone to provide me with alerts to keep me on schedule.
Realistic	Improving my confidence in statistics is really important, as it will help me understand the findings of key psychological research studies. Understanding the findings will give me more scope to critique the literature and achieve better marks. Having a good foundation in applying statistics will also help me when it comes to designing my dissertation project.
Timebound	By the end of this module I will have achieved at least a B grade (2:1).

Index

Page numbers in italics are figures; with 't' are tables.